T0116436

Thriving
TO 50 AND BEYOND
JOURNAL

making the rest of your life the best part of your life,
starts with creating a really good day

Shannon Blas

BALBOA.PRESS
A DIVISION OF HAY HOUSE

Balboa Press books may be ordered through booksellers or by contacting:

Balboa Press
A Division of Hay House
1663 Liberty Drive
Bloomington, IN 47403
www.balboapress.com
844-682-1282

Because of the dynamic nature of the Internet, any web addresses or links contained in this book may have changed since publication and may no longer be valid. The views expressed in this work are solely those of the author and do not necessarily reflect the views of the publisher, and the publisher hereby disclaims any responsibility for them.

The author of this book does not dispense medical advice or prescribe the use of any technique as a form of treatment for physical, emotional, or medical problems without the advice of a physician, either directly or indirectly. The intent of the author is only to offer information of a general nature to help you in your quest for emotional and spiritual well-being. In the event you use any of the information in this book for yourself, which is your constitutional right, the author and the publisher assume no responsibility for your actions.

Any people depicted in stock imagery provided by Getty Images are models, and such images are being used for illustrative purposes only. Certain stock imagery © Getty Images.

Print information available on the last page.

ISBN: 979-8-7652-4198-1 (sc)
ISBN: 979-8-7652-4200-1 (hc)
ISBN: 979-8-7652-4199-8 (e)

Balboa Press rev. date: 06/12/2023

Welcome to your Thriving to 50 and Beyond Journal. I am so excited that you have decided to be a part of this 90 day journey! As we move into this next chapter of life it is easy to lose our focus. You may spend time looking back with regret and wishing you could change some things OR thinking about the future and worrying. Typically we have more time on our hands, and sometimes we aren't sure what to do with it. Add in our emotions, aka crazy hormones, that can make us feel like we aren't ourselves anymore. It can be an interesting time of life. The purpose of this journal is to embrace this next chapter by being present each day and focusing on the things you can control. What I have found is when you are present and you RUN YOUR DAY with intention vs letting the DAY RUN YOU, you can have a really good day. And when you have a few really good days in a row, that turns into a really good week! Really good weeks turn into really good months, and really good months turn into a really good year! My goal for this journal is for you to start planning to have really good days that lead to making rest of your life the best part of your life.

love,
shannon

defining YOUR REALLY GOOD DAY

Let's start by defining your really good day and break down what that looks like for you. Take a look at the questions below and make some notes on the following page. These notes will give you the outline you need to write down and start creating really good days.

What time do you prefer to get up?
How many hours of sleep do you like to get?
Do you have a morning routine?
Do you workout? If so what do you like to do and what time of day is best for you to workout?
What morning habits make you feel good?
What do you do for personal growth?
What do you like to read, listen to?
What do you like to get done before noon?
What is your ideal day socially?
Who do you like to spend time with?
What do you like to do to add fun into your day?
What are your hobbies?
What does your ideal family time look like?
Do you prefer a busy day with lots going on or a day with less on your calendar?
What do you like to do for meals & snacks? Have a plan or figure it out based on your day?
Any bedtime routines that help you sleep?
What's your ideal bedtime?
Is there a time that you put your phone down and let your mind relax?

defining YOUR REALLY GOOD DAY

NOTES

WORK DAY	NON-WORK DAY

RATE THE ITEMS THAT ARE MOST
IMPORTANT TO YOU

TODAY I AM THRIVING

defining YOUR REALLY GOOD DAY

PICK THE TOP THINGS THAT WILL CREATE YOUR
REALLY GOOD WORK & NON-WORK DAY

WHAT DO YOU WANT TO DO DAILY? WEEKLY?

TODAY I AM THRIVING

sleep... WHERE IT ALL STARTS

Getting enough sleep is critical for our physical and mental health, as well as our performance and well-being. It's so important to prioritize sleep and aim for 7-9 hours of quality sleep each night! Did you know sleep...

- Plays a vital role in repairing and restoring our body: It helps reduce inflammation, lower blood pressure, and strengthen our immune system. Lack of sleep, on the other hand, can lead to a host of physical health problems, including weight gain and chronic diseases.
- Helps with mental clarity and focus: Getting enough sleep helps us think more clearly, make better decisions, and stay focused throughout the day. When we are sleep-deprived, our cognitive function declines, making it harder to concentrate, remember things (brain fog), and solve problems.
- Improves our mood: Sleep is critical for regulating our emotions and mood. A lack of sleep can lead to irritability, anxiety, and even depression. Getting enough sleep helps us feel happier, more energized, and better equipped to handle the day.
- Improves our performance: Sleep helps improve reaction times, coordination, and overall physical performance. It also improves our ability to learn and retain new information.
- Lowers stress levels: Sleep helps regulate our stress hormones, such as cortisol. When we're sleep-deprived, our cortisol levels can remain elevated, leading to chronic stress and its associated health problems.

gratitude...

THE QUALITY OF BEING THANKFUL

Making today and the rest of your life the best part of your life starts with gratitude. Did you know writing down three things you are grateful for every day can shift your entire mental state? Gratitude can:

- Help you feel grounded during challenging times
- Boost your mental health and well being
- Allow your mind to focus on positive things and positive emotions
- Make you more optimistic
- Allow you to recognize and appreciate the simple things in life
- Decrease anxiety and depression
- Strengthen your immune system
- Help you experience more joy and pleasure
- Cause you to feel happier
- Give you a higher sense of self-worth
- Help you be more compassionate, forgiving, helpful and generous

Gratitude will help you fall in love with the life you already have and realize all the little things in life really are the big things. Gratitude is also strongly associated with greater happiness. Practicing daily gratitude allows you to create a habit of seeking and finding the good in your life. The more grateful you are, the more beauty you will see. When you take time to appreciate things in your life you will attract more positive experiences, joy and abundance.

writing... IMPROVE YOUR WELLBEING

In this journal I am providing daily prompts that can help you start journaling and writing; you may want to expand in this area and have a separate journal. Journaling can:

- Reduce stress and anxiety: Writing down your thoughts and feelings can help you process and manage them better, leading to a reduction in stress and anxiety.
- Improve self-awareness: Journaling can help you gain a better understanding of your own thoughts, feelings, and behaviors, which can improve your self-awareness and self-reflection.
- Enhance creativity: Journaling can help stimulate creativity by allowing you to freely express your thoughts and ideas without judgment.
- Boost memory and learning: Writing down important information and reflecting on it in a journal can help you remember it better and reinforce your learning.
- Promote emotional healing: Journaling can be a powerful tool for processing and working through difficult emotions and experiences, leading to emotional healing and growth.
- Increase productivity: Keeping a journal can help you prioritize your tasks and goals, leading to increased productivity and a sense of accomplishment.

plan your day... GET ORGANIZED

Either you RUN YOUR DAY or YOUR DAY RUNS YOU. We clearly don't have control of everything that happens in our day, but if we go into the day with a plan the odds of it being a really good day are much higher than if we go into our day with no plan. Writing down a list of the top 3 things to do each day can be a game changer. Here are a few benefits of planning your day:

- Prioritization: It helps you prioritize your tasks and identify what's most important for you to accomplish in a day. By focusing on the most critical tasks, you can make progress on your goals and feel a sense of accomplishment.
- Organization: It keeps you organized and focused, ensuring that you don't forget anything important. By having a clear plan for the day, you're less likely to get sidetracked or waste time on less important tasks.
- Motivation: It can be motivating to cross things off a to-do list. Seeing your progress throughout the day can give you a sense of satisfaction and motivate you to keep going.

Overall, writing down a list of the top 3 things to do today can help you stay on track, accomplish your goals, and feel more productive and organized. This will help you create a really good day.

movement... SPEND TIME IN NATURE

Did you know getting outside and enjoying nature will also help our mindset and brain health? Make it a point each day to spend time in nature, and you will be amazed at how it can change your state of mind. Here are some benefits of getting outdoors:

- Improves your mood
- Reduces feelings of stress and anger
- Boosts your immune system
- Lowers blood pressure and stress hormone levels
- Improves your sleep
- Slows down the pace of life and causes you to be more present
- Makes you feel happier and more content

Did you know earthing (also know as grounding) refers to bodily contact with the earth? Examples include walking with bare feet on grass, lying in the sand or swimming in the ocean. It's allowing the bottom of your feet, the palms of your hands or your entire body to touch the earth. Doing this can reduce inflammation, pain and stress, improve blood flow, energy and sleep, and generate a greater sense of well being.

movement... BUILD MORE MUSCLE

Research has found that individuals can lose between 3% and 8% of their muscle mass per decade after the age of 30. During menopause, the decline in estrogen levels can lead to a loss of lean muscle mass, along with an increase in body fat. However, regular physical activity and strength training can help prevent or reverse this muscle loss. Resistance training exercises, such as lifting heavier weights or using resistance bands, can help maintain and increase muscle mass.

High-intensity interval training (HIIT) is a type of exercise that involves short bursts of intense activity followed by periods of rest or low-intensity activity. HIIT during menopause can improve cardiovascular health, increase muscle mass, boost metabolism, reduce depression or anxiety symptoms, and improve bone density. However, it may not be suitable for everyone, and women should speak with their healthcare provider before starting a new exercise program.

fuel your body...
MAKE FOOD YOUR MEDICINE

- Do you have weight around your midsection, feel bloated or sluggish, have trouble focusing, experience aches & pains or have trouble sleeping? Many times we can overlook one of the most simple and effective tools we have that affects how we feel. It's the food we eat. Food can be one of the most powerful forms of medicine we have.
- Inflammation is our body's reaction to stress; this stress can come from our environment, our diet, parasites, bacterial or viral infections, and other sources. Think about when you cut yourself; that area becomes inflamed and red but it will eventually heal. However, when your body is inflamed from your diet for long periods of time you start to have symptoms and even chronic disease. Many doctors will prescribe medication and not even address what you are eating. Some of the biggest culprits of inflammation are processed foods, gluten, dairy and sugar. When we add our changing hormones into the formula it becomes even more important to focus on how we are fueling our bodies.

Over the course of these 90 days think of the food you are fueling your body with as medicine. Each time we eat we are telling our bodies how to feel so definitely make choices that make you feel good.

fuel your body...
MAKE FOOD YOUR MEDICINE

Here are some key areas we will focus on each day and include in our journal:

- Have PROTEIN every time you eat. We lose muscle as we age, so we need to make sure we are eating enough protein to build more lean tissue.
- Eat a variety of COLORFUL fruits and vegetables each day. The more colors the more phytonutrients, vitamins and minerals to build a healthier body.
- Drink more WATER. Water restores your energy, will help your skin glow and allows your digestive system to work properly. Many times we think we are drinking more than we actually are, so this is why it's so important to track.
- Increase UNPROCESSED foods. Focus on decreasing processed foods and eating more whole food. A good question to ask is, "can I recreate this in my kitchen?"
- Eat THROUGHOUT the day to reduce cravings at night.
- Give your body a food rest 2-3 HOURS before bed so your body can focus on repairing, restoring and burning fat vs digesting food while you sleep.

reflection...
WAS TODAY A REALLY GOOD DAY?

Reflecting on your day is important for personal growth and well-being because it allows you to learn from experiences, improve self-awareness, celebrate achievements, manage emotions, strengthen relationships, and set goals. Let's take a closer look at each of these areas.

- Learn from your experiences: Looking back at your day will allow you to identify what worked well and what didn't. This helps you learn from your experiences and make tomorrow even better.
- Improve your self-awareness: Reflection helps you understand your thoughts, feelings, and behaviors better. This can help you recognize patterns in your day and where you want to make changes.
- Celebrate your achievements: Reflecting on your day allows you to celebrate your achievements, no matter how small. This boosts your confidence, motivation and overall sense of well-being.
- Manage your emotions: Reflection can help you process your emotions. It can also help you identify triggers and help you develop coping strategies and come up with ways to reduce your stress.
- Strengthen your relationships: Looking back at your day can help you recognize how your actions impact others.
- Set goals: Reflecting on your day can help you identify areas where you want to improve. This can help you set goals and make progress towards creating your version of a really good day.

date _____

WHEN YOU FOCUS ON THE GOOD
THE GOOD GETS BETTER

- ESTER HICKS

HOW MUCH SLEEP DID I GET LAST NIGHT? _____

i am so grateful...

3 THINGS I AM GRATEFUL FOR TODAY

1. _____
2. _____
3. _____

a really good day today includes..

_____
_____
_____
_____

today's priorities...

3 MOST IMPORTANT THINGS TO DO TODAY:

1. _____
2. _____
3. _____

TODAY I AM THRIVING

evening check in

movement

HOW DID I MOVE TODAY? ....

    WEIGHTS❑ HIIT WORKOUT❑ ENJOYED NATURE❑ OTHER❑

HOW WAS MY ENERGY LEVEL TODAY? ....

....

....

....

....

fuel

❑ PROTEIN WITH EACH MEAL
❑ COLOR WITH EACH MEAL
WHAT COLORS DID I EAT TODAY? ....
WATER INTAKE.. HOW MANY OUNCES DID I DRINK TODAY? ....
❑ GAVE MY BODY A FOOD REST BEFORE BED SO IT IS ABLE TO FOCUS
ON RESTORING AND REPAIRING WHILE I SLEEP

reflection

    WAS THIS A REALLY GOOD DAY? WHAT DID I LOVE ABOUT
TODAY? WHAT DO I WANT TO BE BETTER WITH TOMORROW?

....

....

....

....

TODAY I AM THRIVING

date _____

TWO THINGS YOU CAN CONTROL IN LIFE
ARE YOUR ATTITUDE AND YOUR EFFORT.

-BILLY COX

HOW MUCH SLEEP DID I GET LAST NIGHT? _____

i am so grateful...

3 THINGS I AM GRATEFUL FOR TODAY

1. _____
2. _____
3. _____

today i want to be more...

_____

_____

_____

_____

today's priorities...

3 MOST IMPORTANT THINGS TO DO TODAY:

1. _____
2. _____
3. _____

evening check in

movement

HOW DID I MOVE TODAY? ....

    WEIGHTS❑ HIIT WORKOUT❑ ENJOYED NATURE❑ OTHER❑

HOW WAS MY ENERGY LEVEL TODAY? ....

....

....

....

....

fuel

❑ PROTEIN WITH EACH MEAL
❑ COLOR WITH EACH MEAL
WHAT COLORS DID I EAT TODAY? ....
WATER INTAKE.. HOW MANY OUNCES DID I DRINK TODAY? ....
❑ GAVE MY BODY A FOOD REST BEFORE BED SO IT IS ABLE TO FOCUS
ON RESTORING AND REPAIRING WHILE I SLEEP

reflection

    WAS THIS A REALLY GOOD DAY? WHAT DID I LOVE ABOUT
TODAY? WHAT DO I WANT TO BE BETTER WITH TOMORROW?

....

....

....

....

TODAY I AM THRIVING

date _____

FOCUS ON THE STEP IN FRONT OF
YOU NOT THE WHOLE STAIRCASE
- UNKNOWN

HOW MUCH SLEEP DID I GET LAST NIGHT?_____

i am so grateful...
3 THINGS I AM GRATEFUL FOR TODAY

1. _____
2. _____
3. _____

i like me best when...

_____
_____
_____
_____

today's priorities...
3 MOST IMPORTANT THINGS TO DO TODAY:

1. _____
2. _____
3. _____

evening check in

movement

HOW DID I MOVE TODAY? ....

WEIGHTS❑ HIIT WORKOUT❑ ENJOYED NATURE❑ OTHER❑

HOW WAS MY ENERGY LEVEL TODAY? ....

....

....

....

....

fuel

❑ PROTEIN WITH EACH MEAL
❑ COLOR WITH EACH MEAL
WHAT COLORS DID I EAT TODAY? ....
WATER INTAKE.. HOW MANY OUNCES DID I DRINK TODAY? ....
❑ GAVE MY BODY A FOOD REST BEFORE BED SO IT IS ABLE TO FOCUS
ON RESTORING AND REPAIRING WHILE I SLEEP

reflection

WAS THIS A REALLY GOOD DAY? WHAT DID I LOVE ABOUT
TODAY? WHAT DO I WANT TO BE BETTER WITH TOMORROW?

....

....

....

....

TODAY I AM THRIVING

date _____

A NEGATIVE MIND WILL NEVER
GIVE YOU A POSITIVE LIFE

- ZIAD K ABELNOUR

HOW MUCH SLEEP DID I GET LAST NIGHT?_____

i am so grateful...

3 THINGS I AM GRATEFUL FOR TODAY

1. _____
2. _____
3. _____

the best version of me is...

_____

_____

_____

_____

_____

today's priorities...

3 MOST IMPORTANT THINGS TO DO TODAY:

1. _____
2. _____
3. _____

TODAY I AM THRIVING

evening check in

movement

HOW DID I MOVE TODAY? _____

WEIGHTS❑ HIIT WORKOUT❑ ENJOYED NATURE❑ OTHER❑

HOW WAS MY ENERGY LEVEL TODAY? _____

_____
_____
_____
_____

fuel

❑ PROTEIN WITH EACH MEAL
❑ COLOR WITH EACH MEAL
WHAT COLORS DID I EAT TODAY? _____
WATER INTAKE.. HOW MANY OUNCES DID I DRINK TODAY? _____
❑ GAVE MY BODY A FOOD REST BEFORE BED SO IT IS ABLE TO FOCUS
ON RESTORING AND REPAIRING WHILE I SLEEP

reflection

WAS THIS A REALLY GOOD DAY? WHAT DID I LOVE ABOUT
TODAY? WHAT DO I WANT TO BE BETTER WITH TOMORROW?

_____
_____
_____
_____

date _____

BE THE REASON SOMEONE SMILES TODAY.
- ROY T BENNETT

HOW MUCH SLEEP DID I GET LAST NIGHT? _____

i am so grateful...
3 THINGS I AM GRATEFUL FOR TODAY

1. _____
2. _____
3. _____

in 90 days i want...

_____

_____

_____

_____

today's priorities...
3 MOST IMPORTANT THINGS TO DO TODAY:

1. _____
2. _____
3. _____

evening check in

movement

HOW DID I MOVE TODAY? ....

WEIGHTS❏ HIIT WORKOUT❏ ENJOYED NATURE❏ OTHER❏

HOW WAS MY ENERGY LEVEL TODAY? ....

....

....

....

....

fuel

❏ PROTEIN WITH EACH MEAL
❏ COLOR WITH EACH MEAL
WHAT COLORS DID I EAT TODAY? ....
WATER INTAKE.. HOW MANY OUNCES DID I DRINK TODAY? ....
❏ GAVE MY BODY A FOOD REST BEFORE BED SO IT IS ABLE TO FOCUS
ON RESTORING AND REPAIRING WHILE I SLEEP

reflection

WAS THIS A REALLY GOOD DAY? WHAT DID I LOVE ABOUT
TODAY? WHAT DO I WANT TO BE BETTER WITH TOMORROW?

....

....

....

....

TODAY I AM THRIVING

date _____

NEVER LET YOUR FEAR DECIDE YOUR FATE
- AARON BRUNO

HOW MUCH SLEEP DID I GET LAST NIGHT? _____

i am so grateful...
3 THINGS I AM GRATEFUL FOR TODAY

1. _____
2. _____
3. _____

today my main focus is...

_____
_____
_____
_____

today's priorities...
3 MOST IMPORTANT THINGS TO DO TODAY:

1. _____
2. _____
3. _____

evening check in

movement

HOW DID I MOVE TODAY? ....

WEIGHTS❏ HIIT WORKOUT❏ ENJOYED NATURE❏ OTHER❏

HOW WAS MY ENERGY LEVEL TODAY? ....

....
....
....
....

fuel

❏ PROTEIN WITH EACH MEAL
❏ COLOR WITH EACH MEAL
WHAT COLORS DID I EAT TODAY? ....
WATER INTAKE.. HOW MANY OUNCES DID I DRINK TODAY? ....
❏ GAVE MY BODY A FOOD REST BEFORE BED SO IT IS ABLE TO FOCUS
ON RESTORING AND REPAIRING WHILE I SLEEP

reflection

WAS THIS A REALLY GOOD DAY? WHAT DID I LOVE ABOUT
TODAY? WHAT DO I WANT TO BE BETTER WITH TOMORROW?

....
....
....
....

TODAY I AM THRIVING

date ———————————————————————

TRUST THE TIMING OF YOUR LIFE
-- BRITTANY BURGUNDER

HOW MUCH SLEEP DID I GET LAST NIGHT? ....

i am so grateful...
3 THINGS I AM GRATEFUL FOR TODAY

1. ....
2. ....
3. ....

what am i happy about...

....

....

....

....

today's priorities...
3 MOST IMPORTANT THINGS TO DO TODAY:

1. ....
2. ....
3. ....

TODAY I AM THRIVING

evening check in

movement

HOW DID I MOVE TODAY? ....

WEIGHTS❑ HIIT WORKOUT❑ ENJOYED NATURE❑ OTHER❑

HOW WAS MY ENERGY LEVEL TODAY? ....

....

....

....

....

fuel

❑ PROTEIN WITH EACH MEAL
❑ COLOR WITH EACH MEAL
WHAT COLORS DID I EAT TODAY? ....
WATER INTAKE.. HOW MANY OUNCES DID I DRINK TODAY? ....
❑ GAVE MY BODY A FOOD REST BEFORE BED SO IT IS ABLE TO FOCUS
ON RESTORING AND REPAIRING WHILE I SLEEP

reflection

WAS THIS A REALLY GOOD DAY? WHAT DID I LOVE ABOUT
TODAY? WHAT DO I WANT TO BE BETTER WITH TOMORROW?

....

....

....

....

TODAY I AM THRIVING

weekly reflection

HOW MANY REALLY GOOD DAYS DID I HAVE THIS WEEK? WHAT DO I WANT TO WORK ON NEXT WEEK?

date _____

IT IS YOUR STORY. MAKE IT A GOOD ONE

- UNKNOWN

HOW MUCH SLEEP DID I GET LAST NIGHT? _____

i am so grateful...

3 THINGS I AM GRATEFUL FOR TODAY

1. _____
2. _____
3. _____

what am i excited for...

_____
_____
_____
_____

today's priorities...

3 MOST IMPORTANT THINGS TO DO TODAY:

1. _____
2. _____
3. _____

TODAY I AM THRIVING

evening check in

movement

HOW DID I MOVE TODAY? ....

WEIGHTS❏ HIIT WORKOUT❏ ENJOYED NATURE❏ OTHER❏

HOW WAS MY ENERGY LEVEL TODAY? _____

fuel

❏ PROTEIN WITH EACH MEAL
❏ COLOR WITH EACH MEAL
WHAT COLORS DID I EAT TODAY? _____
WATER INTAKE.. HOW MANY OUNCES DID I DRINK TODAY? _____
❏ GAVE MY BODY A FOOD REST BEFORE BED SO IT IS ABLE TO FOCUS
ON RESTORING AND REPAIRING WHILE I SLEEP

reflection

WAS THIS A REALLY GOOD DAY? WHAT DID I LOVE ABOUT
TODAY? WHAT DO I WANT TO BE BETTER WITH TOMORROW?

TODAY I AM THRIVING

date —————————————————————

MAKE TODAY SO AWESOME
YESTERDAY GETS JEALOUS

- AVANI SHARMA

HOW MUCH SLEEP DID I GET LAST NIGHT?————————

i am so grateful...

3 THINGS I AM GRATEFUL FOR TODAY

1. ————————————————————————
2. ————————————————————————
3. ————————————————————————

what new thing do i want to do today...

————————————————————————

————————————————————————

————————————————————————

————————————————————————

today's priorities...

3 MOST IMPORTANT THINGS TO DO TODAY:

1. ————————————————————————
2. ————————————————————————
3. ————————————————————————

TODAY I AM THRIVING

evening check in

movement

HOW DID I MOVE TODAY? ....

WEIGHTS❑ HIIT WORKOUT❑ ENJOYED NATURE❑ OTHER❑

HOW WAS MY ENERGY LEVEL TODAY? _____

---

fuel

❑ PROTEIN WITH EACH MEAL
❑ COLOR WITH EACH MEAL
WHAT COLORS DID I EAT TODAY? _____
WATER INTAKE.. HOW MANY OUNCES DID I DRINK TODAY? ....
❑ GAVE MY BODY A FOOD REST BEFORE BED SO IT IS ABLE TO FOCUS
ON RESTORING AND REPAIRING WHILE I SLEEP

reflection

WAS THIS A REALLY GOOD DAY? WHAT DID I LOVE ABOUT
TODAY? WHAT DO I WANT TO BE BETTER WITH TOMORROW?

TODAY I AM THRIVING

date _____

VISUALIZE YOUR HIGHEST SELF AND
START SHOWING UP AS HER

- ANITA QUANSAH LONDON

HOW MUCH SLEEP DID I GET LAST NIGHT? _____

i am so grateful...

3 THINGS I AM GRATEFUL FOR TODAY

1. _____
2. _____
3. _____

what am i committed to today...

_____

_____

_____

_____

today's priorities...

3 MOST IMPORTANT THINGS TO DO TODAY:

1. _____
2. _____
3. _____

TODAY I AM THRIVING

evening check in

movement

HOW DID I MOVE TODAY? ....

WEIGHTS❑ HIIT WORKOUT❑ ENJOYED NATURE❑ OTHER❑

HOW WAS MY ENERGY LEVEL TODAY? ....

....
....
....
....

fuel

❑ PROTEIN WITH EACH MEAL
❑ COLOR WITH EACH MEAL
WHAT COLORS DID I EAT TODAY? ....
WATER INTAKE.. HOW MANY OUNCES DID I DRINK TODAY? ....
❑ GAVE MY BODY A FOOD REST BEFORE BED SO IT IS ABLE TO FOCUS
ON RESTORING AND REPAIRING WHILE I SLEEP

reflection

WAS THIS A REALLY GOOD DAY? WHAT DID I LOVE ABOUT
TODAY? WHAT DO I WANT TO BE BETTER WITH TOMORROW?

....
....
....
....

TODAY I AM THRIVING

date _____

I TRUST THE NEXT CHAPTER
BECAUSE I KNOW THE AUTHOR

- UNKNOWN

HOW MUCH SLEEP DID I GET LAST NIGHT?_____

i am so grateful...

3 THINGS I AM GRATEFUL FOR TODAY

1. _____
2. _____
3. _____

who and what do i love...

_____

_____

_____

_____

today's priorities...

3 MOST IMPORTANT THINGS TO DO TODAY:

1. _____
2. _____
3. _____

TODAY I AM THRIVING

evening check in

movement

HOW DID I MOVE TODAY? ....

WEIGHTS❑ HIIT WORKOUT❑ ENJOYED NATURE❑ OTHER❑

HOW WAS MY ENERGY LEVEL TODAY? _____

....
....
....
....

fuel

❑ PROTEIN WITH EACH MEAL
❑ COLOR WITH EACH MEAL
WHAT COLORS DID I EAT TODAY? _____
WATER INTAKE.. HOW MANY OUNCES DID I DRINK TODAY? ....
❑ GAVE MY BODY A FOOD REST BEFORE BED SO IT IS ABLE TO FOCUS
ON RESTORING AND REPAIRING WHILE I SLEEP

reflection

WAS THIS A REALLY GOOD DAY? WHAT DID I LOVE ABOUT
TODAY? WHAT DO I WANT TO BE BETTER WITH TOMORROW?

....
....
....
....

TODAY I AM THRIVING

date _____

EITHER YOU RUN THE DAY, OR THE
DAY RUNS YOU. YOU CHOOSE

- JIM ROHN

HOW MUCH SLEEP DID I GET LAST NIGHT? _____

i am so grateful...

3 THINGS I AM GRATEFUL FOR TODAY

1. _____
2. _____
3. _____

what am i proud of...

_____
_____
_____
_____

today's priorities...

3 MOST IMPORTANT THINGS TO DO TODAY:

1. _____
2. _____
3. _____

evening check in ———————————————

movement

HOW DID I MOVE TODAY? ....

WEIGHTS❑ HIIT WORKOUT❑ ENJOYED NATURE❑ OTHER❑

HOW WAS MY ENERGY LEVEL TODAY? _____

....
....
....
....

fuel

❑ PROTEIN WITH EACH MEAL
❑ COLOR WITH EACH MEAL
WHAT COLORS DID I EAT TODAY? _____
WATER INTAKE.. HOW MANY OUNCES DID I DRINK TODAY? ....
❑ GAVE MY BODY A FOOD REST BEFORE BED SO IT IS ABLE TO FOCUS
ON RESTORING AND REPAIRING WHILE I SLEEP

reflection

WAS THIS A REALLY GOOD DAY? WHAT DID I LOVE ABOUT
TODAY? WHAT DO I WANT TO BE BETTER WITH TOMORROW?

....
....
....
....

TODAY I AM THRIVING

date _____

BE THE KIND OF PERSON THAT MAKES OTHERS WANT TO UP THEIR GAME

- UNKNOWN

HOW MUCH SLEEP DID I GET LAST NIGHT? _____

i am so grateful...

3 THINGS I AM GRATEFUL FOR TODAY

1. _____
2. _____
3. _____

what is one thing i want to change...

_____

_____

_____

_____

today's priorities...

3 MOST IMPORTANT THINGS TO DO TODAY:

1. _____
2. _____
3. _____

evening check in

movement

HOW DID I MOVE TODAY? ....

WEIGHTS❑ HIIT WORKOUT❑ ENJOYED NATURE❑ OTHER❑

HOW WAS MY ENERGY LEVEL TODAY? ....

fuel

❑ PROTEIN WITH EACH MEAL
❑ COLOR WITH EACH MEAL
WHAT COLORS DID I EAT TODAY? ....
WATER INTAKE.. HOW MANY OUNCES DID I DRINK TODAY? ....
❑ GAVE MY BODY A FOOD REST BEFORE BED SO IT IS ABLE TO FOCUS
ON RESTORING AND REPAIRING WHILE I SLEEP

reflection

WAS THIS A REALLY GOOD DAY? WHAT DID I LOVE ABOUT
TODAY? WHAT DO I WANT TO BE BETTER WITH TOMORROW?

date _____

IMAGINE WHERE YOU WILL BE A YEAR
FROM NOW IF YOU START TODAY

- UNKNOWN

HOW MUCH SLEEP DID I GET LAST NIGHT?_____

i am so grateful...

3 THINGS I AM GRATEFUL FOR TODAY

1. _____
2. _____
3. _____

what am i currently enjoying in my life...

_____
_____
_____
_____

today's priorities...

3 MOST IMPORTANT THINGS TO DO TODAY:

1. _____
2. _____
3. _____

evening check in

movement

HOW DID I MOVE TODAY? ....

WEIGHTS❑ HIIT WORKOUT❑ ENJOYED NATURE❑ OTHER❑

HOW WAS MY ENERGY LEVEL TODAY? _____

....
....
....
....

fuel

❑ PROTEIN WITH EACH MEAL
❑ COLOR WITH EACH MEAL
WHAT COLORS DID I EAT TODAY? _____
WATER INTAKE.. HOW MANY OUNCES DID I DRINK TODAY? _____
❑ GAVE MY BODY A FOOD REST BEFORE BED SO IT IS ABLE TO FOCUS
ON RESTORING AND REPAIRING WHILE I SLEEP

reflection

WAS THIS A REALLY GOOD DAY? WHAT DID I LOVE ABOUT
TODAY? WHAT DO I WANT TO BE BETTER WITH TOMORROW?

....
....
....
....

TODAY I AM THRIVING

weekly reflection

HOW MANY REALLY GOOD DAYS DID I HAVE THIS WEEK? WHAT DO I WANT TO WORK ON NEXT WEEK?

date _____

LIFE IS 10% WHAT HAPPENS TO YOU
AND 90% HOW YOU REACT TO IT
- CHARLES R SWINDOLL

HOW MUCH SLEEP DID I GET LAST NIGHT?_____

i am so grateful...
3 THINGS I AM GRATEFUL FOR TODAY

1. _____
2. _____
3. _____

what is the best version of me...

_____
_____
_____
_____

today's priorities...
3 MOST IMPORTANT THINGS TO DO TODAY:

1. _____
2. _____
3. _____

evening check in

movement

HOW DID I MOVE TODAY? ....

    WEIGHTS☐ HIIT WORKOUT☐ ENJOYED NATURE☐ OTHER☐

HOW WAS MY ENERGY LEVEL TODAY? ....

....

....

....

....

fuel

☐ PROTEIN WITH EACH MEAL
☐ COLOR WITH EACH MEAL
WHAT COLORS DID I EAT TODAY? ....
WATER INTAKE.. HOW MANY OUNCES DID I DRINK TODAY? ....
☐ GAVE MY BODY A FOOD REST BEFORE BED SO IT IS ABLE TO FOCUS
ON RESTORING AND REPAIRING WHILE I SLEEP

reflection

    WAS THIS A REALLY GOOD DAY? WHAT DID I LOVE ABOUT
TODAY? WHAT DO I WANT TO BE BETTER WITH TOMORROW?

....

....

....

....

TODAY I AM THRIVING

date _____

LIFE HAPPENS WHEN YOU STOP
WAITING FOR THE PERFECT TIME

- UNKNOWN

HOW MUCH SLEEP DID I GET LAST NIGHT? _____

i am so grateful...

3 THINGS I AM GRATEFUL FOR TODAY

1. _____
2. _____
3. _____

what do i need to do today to be more present...

_____
_____
_____
_____

today's priorities...

3 MOST IMPORTANT THINGS TO DO TODAY:

1. _____
2. _____
3. _____

TODAY I AM THRIVING

evening check in

movement

HOW DID I MOVE TODAY? ....

    WEIGHTS❏ HIIT WORKOUT❏ ENJOYED NATURE❏ OTHER❏

HOW WAS MY ENERGY LEVEL TODAY? ....

....

....

....

....

fuel

❏ PROTEIN WITH EACH MEAL
❏ COLOR WITH EACH MEAL
WHAT COLORS DID I EAT TODAY? ....
WATER INTAKE.. HOW MANY OUNCES DID I DRINK TODAY? ....
❏ GAVE MY BODY A FOOD REST BEFORE BED SO IT IS ABLE TO FOCUS
ON RESTORING AND REPAIRING WHILE I SLEEP

reflection

    WAS THIS A REALLY GOOD DAY? WHAT DID I LOVE ABOUT
TODAY? WHAT DO I WANT TO BE BETTER WITH TOMORROW?

....

....

....

....

date _____

NEVER UNDERESTIMATE THE POWER OF A KIND WOMAN. KINDNESS IS A CHOICE THAT COMES FROM INCREDIBLE STRENGTH

– HILARY ROBERTS

HOW MUCH SLEEP DID I GET LAST NIGHT?_____

i am so grateful...
3 THINGS I AM GRATEFUL FOR TODAY

1. _____
2. _____
3. _____

what are my favorites things to do...

_____

_____

_____

_____

today's priorities...
3 MOST IMPORTANT THINGS TO DO TODAY:

1. _____
2. _____
3. _____

TODAY I AM THRIVING

evening check in

movement

HOW DID I MOVE TODAY? ....

WEIGHTS❑ HIIT WORKOUT❑ ENJOYED NATURE❑ OTHER❑

HOW WAS MY ENERGY LEVEL TODAY? ....

....

....

....

....

fuel

❑ PROTEIN WITH EACH MEAL
❑ COLOR WITH EACH MEAL
WHAT COLORS DID I EAT TODAY? ....
WATER INTAKE.. HOW MANY OUNCES DID I DRINK TODAY? ....
❑ GAVE MY BODY A FOOD REST BEFORE BED SO IT IS ABLE TO FOCUS
ON RESTORING AND REPAIRING WHILE I SLEEP

reflection

WAS THIS A REALLY GOOD DAY? WHAT DID I LOVE ABOUT
TODAY? WHAT DO I WANT TO BE BETTER WITH TOMORROW?

....

....

....

....

date —————————————————————————

EACH DAY IS AN OPPORTUNITY FOR JOY

- UNKNOWN

HOW MUCH SLEEP DID I GET LAST NIGHT? ....

i am so grateful...

3 THINGS I AM GRATEFUL FOR TODAY

1. ....
2. ....
3. ....

what inspires me?

....

....

....

....

today's priorities...

3 MOST IMPORTANT THINGS TO DO TODAY:

1. ....
2. ....
3. ....

TODAY I AM THRIVING

evening check in

movement

HOW DID I MOVE TODAY? ....

WEIGHTS❑ HIIT WORKOUT❑ ENJOYED NATURE❑ OTHER❑

HOW WAS MY ENERGY LEVEL TODAY? ....

....

....

....

....

fuel

❑ PROTEIN WITH EACH MEAL
❑ COLOR WITH EACH MEAL
WHAT COLORS DID I EAT TODAY? ....
WATER INTAKE.. HOW MANY OUNCES DID I DRINK TODAY? ....
❑ GAVE MY BODY A FOOD REST BEFORE BED SO IT IS ABLE TO FOCUS
ON RESTORING AND REPAIRING WHILE I SLEEP

reflection

WAS THIS A REALLY GOOD DAY? WHAT DID I LOVE ABOUT
TODAY? WHAT DO I WANT TO BE BETTER WITH TOMORROW?

....

....

....

....

TODAY I AM THRIVING

date _____

THOUGHTS HAVE ENERGY.
MAKE SURE YOURS ARE POSITIVE

- UNKNOWN

HOW MUCH SLEEP DID I GET LAST NIGHT?_____

i am so grateful...

3 THINGS I AM GRATEFUL FOR TODAY

1. _____
2. _____
3. _____

what is on my bucket list...

_____

_____

_____

_____

today's priorities...

3 MOST IMPORTANT THINGS TO DO TODAY:

1. _____
2. _____
3. _____

evening check in

movement

HOW DID I MOVE TODAY? ....

WEIGHTS❏ HIIT WORKOUT❏ ENJOYED NATURE❏ OTHER❏

HOW WAS MY ENERGY LEVEL TODAY? ....

....

....

....

....

fuel

❏ PROTEIN WITH EACH MEAL
❏ COLOR WITH EACH MEAL
WHAT COLORS DID I EAT TODAY? ....
WATER INTAKE.. HOW MANY OUNCES DID I DRINK TODAY? ....
❏ GAVE MY BODY A FOOD REST BEFORE BED SO IT IS ABLE TO FOCUS
ON RESTORING AND REPAIRING WHILE I SLEEP

reflection

WAS THIS A REALLY GOOD DAY? WHAT DID I LOVE ABOUT
TODAY? WHAT DO I WANT TO BE BETTER WITH TOMORROW?

....

....

....

....

TODAY I AM THRIVING

date _____

WORRYING DOES NOT TAKE AWAY TOMORROW'S TROUBLES. IT TAKES AWAY TODAY'S PEACE

-- RANDY ARMSTRONG

HOW MUCH SLEEP DID I GET LAST NIGHT? _____

i am so grateful...
3 THINGS I AM GRATEFUL FOR TODAY

1. _____
2. _____
3. _____

what is one thing i want to work on...

_____
_____
_____
_____

today's priorities...
3 MOST IMPORTANT THINGS TO DO TODAY:

1. _____
2. _____
3. _____

TODAY I AM THRIVING

evening check in

movement

HOW DID I MOVE TODAY? ....

WEIGHTS❑ HIIT WORKOUT❑ ENJOYED NATURE❑ OTHER❑

HOW WAS MY ENERGY LEVEL TODAY? ....

....

....

....

....

fuel

❑ PROTEIN WITH EACH MEAL
❑ COLOR WITH EACH MEAL
WHAT COLORS DID I EAT TODAY? ....
WATER INTAKE.. HOW MANY OUNCES DID I DRINK TODAY? ....
❑ GAVE MY BODY A FOOD REST BEFORE BED SO IT IS ABLE TO FOCUS
ON RESTORING AND REPAIRING WHILE I SLEEP

reflection

WAS THIS A REALLY GOOD DAY? WHAT DID I LOVE ABOUT
TODAY? WHAT DO I WANT TO BE BETTER WITH TOMORROW?

....

....

....

....

TODAY I AM THRIVING

date _____

I AM BECOMING THE BEST
VERSION OF MYSELF

- UNKNOWN

HOW MUCH SLEEP DID I GET LAST NIGHT?_____

i am so grateful...

3 THINGS I AM GRATEFUL FOR TODAY

1. _____
2. _____
3. _____

what are the small things that make me happy...

_____
_____
_____
_____

today's priorities...

3 MOST IMPORTANT THINGS TO DO TODAY:

1. _____
2. _____
3. _____

evening check in

movement

HOW DID I MOVE TODAY? ....

    WEIGHTS☐ HIIT WORKOUT☐ ENJOYED NATURE☐ OTHER☐

HOW WAS MY ENERGY LEVEL TODAY? ....

....
....
....
....

fuel

☐ PROTEIN WITH EACH MEAL
☐ COLOR WITH EACH MEAL
WHAT COLORS DID I EAT TODAY? ....
WATER INTAKE.. HOW MANY OUNCES DID I DRINK TODAY? ....
☐ GAVE MY BODY A FOOD REST BEFORE BED SO IT IS ABLE TO FOCUS
ON RESTORING AND REPAIRING WHILE I SLEEP

reflection

    WAS THIS A REALLY GOOD DAY? WHAT DID I LOVE ABOUT
TODAY? WHAT DO I WANT TO BE BETTER WITH TOMORROW?

....
....
....
....

TODAY I AM THRIVING

weekly reflection

HOW MANY REALLY GOOD DAYS DID I HAVE THIS WEEK? WHAT DO I WANT TO WORK ON NEXT WEEK?

_____

_____

_____

_____

_____

_____

_____

_____

_____

_____

_____

_____

_____

date _____

THE MORE GRATEFUL I AM
THE MORE BEAUTY I SEE

- MARY DAVIS

HOW MUCH SLEEP DID I GET LAST NIGHT?_____

i am so grateful...
3 THINGS I AM GRATEFUL FOR TODAY

1. ....
2. ....
3. ....

what am i proud of...

....

....

....

....

today's priorities...
3 MOST IMPORTANT THINGS TO DO TODAY:

1. ....
2. ....
3. ....

evening check in

movement

HOW DID I MOVE TODAY? ....

WEIGHTS❏ HIIT WORKOUT❏ ENJOYED NATURE❏ OTHER❏

HOW WAS MY ENERGY LEVEL TODAY? ....

....

....

....

....

fuel

❏ PROTEIN WITH EACH MEAL
❏ COLOR WITH EACH MEAL
WHAT COLORS DID I EAT TODAY? _____
WATER INTAKE.. HOW MANY OUNCES DID I DRINK TODAY? ....
❏ GAVE MY BODY A FOOD REST BEFORE BED SO IT IS ABLE TO FOCUS
ON RESTORING AND REPAIRING WHILE I SLEEP

reflection

WAS THIS A REALLY GOOD DAY? WHAT DID I LOVE ABOUT
TODAY? WHAT DO I WANT TO BE BETTER WITH TOMORROW?

....

....

....

....

TODAY I AM THRIVING

date ——————————————————————————

TAKE TIME TO MAKE YOUR SOUL HAPPY

- JEREMY MCGILVERY

HOW MUCH SLEEP DID I GET LAST NIGHT?..

i am so grateful...

3 THINGS I AM GRATEFUL FOR TODAY

1. ....
2. ....
3. ....

what is most important to me right now?

....

....

....

....

today's priorities...

3 MOST IMPORTANT THINGS TO DO TODAY:

1. ....
2. ....
3. ....

evening check in

movement

HOW DID I MOVE TODAY? ....

WEIGHTS❑ HIIT WORKOUT❑ ENJOYED NATURE❑ OTHER❑

HOW WAS MY ENERGY LEVEL TODAY? ....

....

....

....

....

fuel

❑ PROTEIN WITH EACH MEAL
❑ COLOR WITH EACH MEAL
WHAT COLORS DID I EAT TODAY? ....
WATER INTAKE.. HOW MANY OUNCES DID I DRINK TODAY? ....
❑ GAVE MY BODY A FOOD REST BEFORE BED SO IT IS ABLE TO FOCUS
ON RESTORING AND REPAIRING WHILE I SLEEP

reflection

WAS THIS A REALLY GOOD DAY? WHAT DID I LOVE ABOUT
TODAY? WHAT DO I WANT TO BE BETTER WITH TOMORROW?

....

....

....

....

TODAY I AM THRIVING

date ——————————————————————————

MY FAVORITE AGE IS NOW

- KIRSTEN DUNST

HOW MUCH SLEEP DID I GET LAST NIGHT? ....

i am so grateful...

3 THINGS I AM GRATEFUL FOR TODAY

1. ....
2. ....
3. ....

what am i currently enjoying?

....

....

....

....

today's priorities...

3 MOST IMPORTANT THINGS TO DO TODAY:

1. ....
2. ....
3. ....

TODAY I AM THRIVING

evening check in

movement

HOW DID I MOVE TODAY? ....

WEIGHTS❑ HIIT WORKOUT❑ ENJOYED NATURE❑ OTHER❑

HOW WAS MY ENERGY LEVEL TODAY? _____

....

....

....

....

fuel

❑ PROTEIN WITH EACH MEAL
❑ COLOR WITH EACH MEAL
WHAT COLORS DID I EAT TODAY? _____
WATER INTAKE.. HOW MANY OUNCES DID I DRINK TODAY? ....
❑ GAVE MY BODY A FOOD REST BEFORE BED SO IT IS ABLE TO FOCUS
ON RESTORING AND REPAIRING WHILE I SLEEP

reflection

WAS THIS A REALLY GOOD DAY? WHAT DID I LOVE ABOUT
TODAY? WHAT DO I WANT TO BE BETTER WITH TOMORROW?

....

....

....

....

TODAY I AM THRIVING

date _____

YOU ARE POWERFUL, BEAUTIFUL, BRILLIANT AND BRAVE

- JESSICA MCCORMICK

HOW MUCH SLEEP DID I GET LAST NIGHT? _____

i am so grateful...

3 THINGS I AM GRATEFUL FOR TODAY

1. _____
2. _____
3. _____

what do you think about your daily habits right now?

_____

_____

_____

_____

today's priorities...

3 MOST IMPORTANT THINGS TO DO TODAY:

1. _____
2. _____
3. _____

TODAY I AM THRIVING

evening check in

movement

HOW DID I MOVE TODAY? ....

WEIGHTS❏ HIIT WORKOUT❏ ENJOYED NATURE❏ OTHER❏

HOW WAS MY ENERGY LEVEL TODAY? ....

....

....

....

....

fuel

❏ PROTEIN WITH EACH MEAL
❏ COLOR WITH EACH MEAL
WHAT COLORS DID I EAT TODAY? _____
WATER INTAKE.. HOW MANY OUNCES DID I DRINK TODAY? _____
❏ GAVE MY BODY A FOOD REST BEFORE BED SO IT IS ABLE TO FOCUS
ON RESTORING AND REPAIRING WHILE I SLEEP

reflection

WAS THIS A REALLY GOOD DAY? WHAT DID I LOVE ABOUT
TODAY? WHAT DO I WANT TO BE BETTER WITH TOMORROW?

....

....

....

....

TODAY I AM THRIVING

date _____

BEING SELECTIVE ABOUT WHO GETS YOUR ENERGY IS SELF CARE. READ THAT AGAIN

- BRIAN WEINER

HOW MUCH SLEEP DID I GET LAST NIGHT? _____

i am so grateful...

3 THINGS I AM GRATEFUL FOR TODAY

1. _____
2. _____
3. _____

what do i want to do differently today...

_____

_____

_____

_____

today's priorities...

3 MOST IMPORTANT THINGS TO DO TODAY:

1. _____
2. _____
3. _____

evening check in

movement

HOW DID I MOVE TODAY? ....

WEIGHTS❏ HIIT WORKOUT❏ ENJOYED NATURE❏ OTHER❏

HOW WAS MY ENERGY LEVEL TODAY? _____

---

fuel

❏ PROTEIN WITH EACH MEAL
❏ COLOR WITH EACH MEAL
WHAT COLORS DID I EAT TODAY? _____
WATER INTAKE.. HOW MANY OUNCES DID I DRINK TODAY? _____
❏ GAVE MY BODY A FOOD REST BEFORE BED SO IT IS ABLE TO FOCUS
ON RESTORING AND REPAIRING WHILE I SLEEP

reflection

WAS THIS A REALLY GOOD DAY? WHAT DID I LOVE ABOUT
TODAY? WHAT DO I WANT TO BE BETTER WITH TOMORROW?

TODAY I AM THRIVING

date _____

YOUR LIFE ONLY GETS BETTER WHEN YOU DO. WORK ON YOURSELF AND THE REST WILL FOLLOW

- UNKNOWN

HOW MUCH SLEEP DID I GET LAST NIGHT? ....

i am so grateful...

3 THINGS I AM GRATEFUL FOR TODAY

1. ....
2. ....
3. ....

how can i practice self care today....

....
....
....
....

today's priorities...

3 MOST IMPORTANT THINGS TO DO TODAY:

1. ....
2. ....
3. ....

evening check in

movement

HOW DID I MOVE TODAY? ....

   WEIGHTS❑ HIIT WORKOUT❑ ENJOYED NATURE❑ OTHER❑

HOW WAS MY ENERGY LEVEL TODAY? _____

....

....

....

....

fuel

❑ PROTEIN WITH EACH MEAL
❑ COLOR WITH EACH MEAL
WHAT COLORS DID I EAT TODAY? _____
WATER INTAKE.. HOW MANY OUNCES DID I DRINK TODAY? ....
❑ GAVE MY BODY A FOOD REST BEFORE BED SO IT IS ABLE TO FOCUS
ON RESTORING AND REPAIRING WHILE I SLEEP

reflection

   WAS THIS A REALLY GOOD DAY? WHAT DID I LOVE ABOUT
   TODAY? WHAT DO I WANT TO BE BETTER WITH TOMORROW?

....

....

....

....

TODAY I AM THRIVING

date _____

WAKE UP WITH A PURPOSE

- UNKNOWN

HOW MUCH SLEEP DID I GET LAST NIGHT? _____

i am so grateful...

3 THINGS I AM GRATEFUL FOR TODAY

1. _____
2. _____
3. _____

what is my purpose today?

_____

_____

_____

_____

today's priorities...

3 MOST IMPORTANT THINGS TO DO TODAY:

1. _____
2. _____
3. _____

evening check in

movement

HOW DID I MOVE TODAY? _____

    WEIGHTS❑ HIIT WORKOUT❑ ENJOYED NATURE❑ OTHER❑

HOW WAS MY ENERGY LEVEL TODAY? _____

_____

_____

_____

_____

fuel

❑ PROTEIN WITH EACH MEAL
❑ COLOR WITH EACH MEAL
WHAT COLORS DID I EAT TODAY? _____
WATER INTAKE.. HOW MANY OUNCES DID I DRINK TODAY? _____
❑ GAVE MY BODY A FOOD REST BEFORE BED SO IT IS ABLE TO FOCUS
ON RESTORING AND REPAIRING WHILE I SLEEP

reflection

WAS THIS A REALLY GOOD DAY? WHAT DID I LOVE ABOUT
TODAY? WHAT DO I WANT TO BE BETTER WITH TOMORROW?

_____

_____

_____

_____

TODAY I AM THRIVING

weekly reflection

HOW MANY REALLY GOOD DAYS DID I HAVE THIS WEEK? WHAT DO I WANT TO WORK ON NEXT WEEK?

date _____

EVERY MORNING YOU HAVE A
NEW OPPORTUNITY TO BECOME
A HAPPIER VERSION OF YOU

-- UNKNOWN

HOW MUCH SLEEP DID I GET LAST NIGHT?

_____

i am so grateful...

3 THINGS I AM GRATEFUL FOR TODAY

1. _____
2. _____
3. _____

what makes me the most happy...

_____
_____
_____

today's priorities...

3 MOST IMPORTANT THINGS TO DO TODAY:

1. _____
2. _____
3. _____

evening check in

movement

HOW DID I MOVE TODAY? ....

    WEIGHTS❏ HIIT WORKOUT❏ ENJOYED NATURE❏ OTHER❏

HOW WAS MY ENERGY LEVEL TODAY? ....

....
....
....
....

fuel

❏ PROTEIN WITH EACH MEAL
❏ COLOR WITH EACH MEAL
WHAT COLORS DID I EAT TODAY? ....
WATER INTAKE.. HOW MANY OUNCES DID I DRINK TODAY? ....
❏ GAVE MY BODY A FOOD REST BEFORE BED SO IT IS ABLE TO FOCUS
ON RESTORING AND REPAIRING WHILE I SLEEP

reflection

    WAS THIS A REALLY GOOD DAY? WHAT DID I LOVE ABOUT
TODAY? WHAT DO I WANT TO BE BETTER WITH TOMORROW?

....
....
....
....

date _____

DIFFICULT ROADS OFTEN LEAD
TO BEAUTIFUL DESTINATIONS

- ZIG ZIGLAR

HOW MUCH SLEEP DID I GET LAST NIGHT?_____

i am so grateful...

3 THINGS I AM GRATEFUL FOR TODAY

1. _____
2. _____
3. _____

what would make my day amazing...

_____
_____
_____
_____

today's priorities...

3 MOST IMPORTANT THINGS TO DO TODAY:

1. _____
2. _____
3. _____

evening check in

movement

HOW DID I MOVE TODAY? ....

WEIGHTS❑ HIIT WORKOUT❑ ENJOYED NATURE❑ OTHER❑

HOW WAS MY ENERGY LEVEL TODAY? ....

....
....
....
....

fuel

❑ PROTEIN WITH EACH MEAL
❑ COLOR WITH EACH MEAL
WHAT COLORS DID I EAT TODAY? ....
WATER INTAKE.. HOW MANY OUNCES DID I DRINK TODAY? ....
❑ GAVE MY BODY A FOOD REST BEFORE BED SO IT IS ABLE TO FOCUS
ON RESTORING AND REPAIRING WHILE I SLEEP

reflection

WAS THIS A REALLY GOOD DAY? WHAT DID I LOVE ABOUT
TODAY? WHAT DO I WANT TO BE BETTER WITH TOMORROW?

....
....
....
....

TODAY I AM THRIVING

date _____

YOU ARE THE MOST VALUABLE
INVESTMENT YOU WILL EVER MAKE
- WARREN BUFFET

HOW MUCH SLEEP DID I GET LAST NIGHT? _____

i am so grateful...
3 THINGS I AM GRATEFUL FOR TODAY

1. _____
2. _____
3. _____

what areas of my health do i need to work on...

_____

_____

_____

_____

today's priorities...
3 MOST IMPORTANT THINGS TO DO TODAY:

1. _____
2. _____
3. _____

evening check in

movement

HOW DID I MOVE TODAY? ....

WEIGHTS❑ HIIT WORKOUT❑ ENJOYED NATURE❑ OTHER❑

HOW WAS MY ENERGY LEVEL TODAY? ....

....

....

....

....

fuel

❑ PROTEIN WITH EACH MEAL
❑ COLOR WITH EACH MEAL
WHAT COLORS DID I EAT TODAY? ....
WATER INTAKE.. HOW MANY OUNCES DID I DRINK TODAY? ....
❑ GAVE MY BODY A FOOD REST BEFORE BED SO IT IS ABLE TO FOCUS
ON RESTORING AND REPAIRING WHILE I SLEEP

reflection

WAS THIS A REALLY GOOD DAY? WHAT DID I LOVE ABOUT
TODAY? WHAT DO I WANT TO BE BETTER WITH TOMORROW?

....

....

....

TODAY I AM THRIVING

date _____

THE TRICK TO AGING
GRACEFULLY IS TO ENJOY IT

- UNKNOWN

HOW MUCH SLEEP DID I GET LAST NIGHT? _____

i am so grateful...

3 THINGS I AM GRATEFUL FOR TODAY

1. _____
2. _____
3. _____

what are some things i enjoy about this stage of life...

_____

_____

_____

_____

today's priorities...

3 MOST IMPORTANT THINGS TO DO TODAY:

1. _____
2. _____
3. _____

TODAY I AM THRIVING

evening check in

movement

HOW DID I MOVE TODAY? ....

WEIGHTS❑ HIIT WORKOUT❑ ENJOYED NATURE❑ OTHER❑

HOW WAS MY ENERGY LEVEL TODAY? _____

....
....
....
....

fuel

❑ PROTEIN WITH EACH MEAL
❑ COLOR WITH EACH MEAL
WHAT COLORS DID I EAT TODAY? ....
WATER INTAKE.. HOW MANY OUNCES DID I DRINK TODAY? ....
❑ GAVE MY BODY A FOOD REST BEFORE BED SO IT IS ABLE TO FOCUS
ON RESTORING AND REPAIRING WHILE I SLEEP

reflection

WAS THIS A REALLY GOOD DAY? WHAT DID I LOVE ABOUT
TODAY? WHAT DO I WANT TO BE BETTER WITH TOMORROW?

....
....
....
....

TODAY I AM THRIVING

date _____

THE MOST WASTED OF DAYS IS
ONE WITHOUT LAUGHTER

- EE CUMMINGS

HOW MUCH SLEEP DID I GET LAST NIGHT?_____

i am so grateful...
3 THINGS I AM GRATEFUL FOR TODAY

1. _____
2. _____
3. _____

what are some of my favorite ways to have fun...

_____
_____
_____
_____

today's priorities...
3 MOST IMPORTANT THINGS TO DO TODAY:

1. _____
2. _____
3. _____

evening check in

movement

HOW DID I MOVE TODAY? ....

WEIGHTS❑ HIIT WORKOUT❑ ENJOYED NATURE❑ OTHER❑

HOW WAS MY ENERGY LEVEL TODAY? _____

_____

_____

_____

_____

fuel

❑ PROTEIN WITH EACH MEAL
❑ COLOR WITH EACH MEAL
WHAT COLORS DID I EAT TODAY? ....
WATER INTAKE.. HOW MANY OUNCES DID I DRINK TODAY? ....
❑ GAVE MY BODY A FOOD REST BEFORE BED SO IT IS ABLE TO FOCUS
ON RESTORING AND REPAIRING WHILE I SLEEP

reflection

WAS THIS A REALLY GOOD DAY? WHAT DID I LOVE ABOUT
TODAY? WHAT DO I WANT TO BE BETTER WITH TOMORROW?

_____

_____

_____

_____

TODAY I AM THRIVING

date _____

YOU CAN DO ANYTHING
BUT NOT EVERYTHING

- DAVID ALLEN

HOW MUCH SLEEP DID I GET LAST NIGHT? _____

i am so grateful...

3 THINGS I AM GRATEFUL FOR TODAY

1. _____
2. _____
3. _____

are there some things i need to start saying no to...

_____
_____
_____
_____

today's priorities...

3 MOST IMPORTANT THINGS TO DO TODAY:

1. _____
2. _____
3. _____

TODAY I AM THRIVING

evening check in

movement

HOW DID I MOVE TODAY? ....

WEIGHTS❑ HIIT WORKOUT❑ ENJOYED NATURE❑ OTHER❑

HOW WAS MY ENERGY LEVEL TODAY? _____

_____

_____

_____

_____

fuel

❑ PROTEIN WITH EACH MEAL
❑ COLOR WITH EACH MEAL
WHAT COLORS DID I EAT TODAY? _____
WATER INTAKE.. HOW MANY OUNCES DID I DRINK TODAY? ....
❑ GAVE MY BODY A FOOD REST BEFORE BED SO IT IS ABLE TO FOCUS
ON RESTORING AND REPAIRING WHILE I SLEEP

reflection

WAS THIS A REALLY GOOD DAY? WHAT DID I LOVE ABOUT
TODAY? WHAT DO I WANT TO BE BETTER WITH TOMORROW?

_____

_____

_____

_____

TODAY I AM THRIVING

date _____

YOUR HEALTH IS AN INVESTMENT,
NOT AN EXPENSE

- JOHN QUELCH

HOW MUCH SLEEP DID I GET LAST NIGHT? _____

i am so grateful...
3 THINGS I AM GRATEFUL FOR TODAY

1. _____
2. _____
3. _____

how do i want to show up today...

_____
_____
_____
_____

today's priorities...
3 MOST IMPORTANT THINGS TO DO TODAY:

1. _____
2. _____
3. _____

TODAY I AM THRIVING

evening check in

movement

HOW DID I MOVE TODAY? ....

WEIGHTS❏ HIIT WORKOUT❏ ENJOYED NATURE❏ OTHER❏

HOW WAS MY ENERGY LEVEL TODAY? ....

....
....
....
....

fuel

❏ PROTEIN WITH EACH MEAL
❏ COLOR WITH EACH MEAL
WHAT COLORS DID I EAT TODAY? ....
WATER INTAKE.. HOW MANY OUNCES DID I DRINK TODAY? ....
❏ GAVE MY BODY A FOOD REST BEFORE BED SO IT IS ABLE TO FOCUS
ON RESTORING AND REPAIRING WHILE I SLEEP

reflection

WAS THIS A REALLY GOOD DAY? WHAT DID I LOVE ABOUT
TODAY? WHAT DO I WANT TO BE BETTER WITH TOMORROW?

....
....
....
....

TODAY I AM THRIVING

weekly reflection

HOW MANY REALLY GOOD DAYS DID I HAVE THIS WEEK? WHAT DO I WANT TO WORK ON NEXT WEEK?

date _____

YOU CAN'T POUR FROM AN EMPTY CUP. TAKE CARE OF YOURSELF FIRST

~ NORM KELLY

HOW MUCH SLEEP DID I GET LAST NIGHT? _____

i am so grateful...

3 THINGS I AM GRATEFUL FOR TODAY

1. ....
2. ....
3. ....

what are some things i need to start doing for myself...

....

....

....

....

today's priorities...

3 MOST IMPORTANT THINGS TO DO TODAY:

1. ....
2. ....
3. ....

TODAY I AM THRIVING

evening check in

movement

HOW DID I MOVE TODAY? ....

WEIGHTS❑ HIIT WORKOUT❑ ENJOYED NATURE❑ OTHER❑

HOW WAS MY ENERGY LEVEL TODAY? ....

....

....

....

....

fuel

❑ PROTEIN WITH EACH MEAL
❑ COLOR WITH EACH MEAL
WHAT COLORS DID I EAT TODAY? ....
WATER INTAKE.. HOW MANY OUNCES DID I DRINK TODAY? ....
❑ GAVE MY BODY A FOOD REST BEFORE BED SO IT IS ABLE TO FOCUS
ON RESTORING AND REPAIRING WHILE I SLEEP

reflection

WAS THIS A REALLY GOOD DAY? WHAT DID I LOVE ABOUT
TODAY? WHAT DO I WANT TO BE BETTER WITH TOMORROW?

....

....

....

....

TODAY I AM THRIVING

date _____

WHATEVER YOU ARE NOT CHANGING, YOU ARE CHOOSING. REMEMBER THAT

- LAURA BUCHANAN

HOW MUCH SLEEP DID I GET LAST NIGHT?_____

i am so grateful...

3 THINGS I AM GRATEFUL FOR TODAY

1. _____
2. _____
3. _____

what are some things i would like to change...

_____

_____

_____

_____

today's priorities...

3 MOST IMPORTANT THINGS TO DO TODAY:

1. _____
2. _____
3. _____

TODAY I AM THRIVING

evening check in

movement

HOW DID I MOVE TODAY? _____

WEIGHTS❑ HIIT WORKOUT❑ ENJOYED NATURE❑ OTHER❑

HOW WAS MY ENERGY LEVEL TODAY? _____

_____
_____
_____
_____

fuel

❑ PROTEIN WITH EACH MEAL
❑ COLOR WITH EACH MEAL
WHAT COLORS DID I EAT TODAY? _____
WATER INTAKE.. HOW MANY OUNCES DID I DRINK TODAY? _____
❑ GAVE MY BODY A FOOD REST BEFORE BED SO IT IS ABLE TO FOCUS
ON RESTORING AND REPAIRING WHILE I SLEEP

reflection

WAS THIS A REALLY GOOD DAY? WHAT DID I LOVE ABOUT
TODAY? WHAT DO I WANT TO BE BETTER WITH TOMORROW?

_____
_____
_____
_____

TODAY I AM THRIVING

date _____

TODAY I WANT YOU TO THINK
ABOUT ALL THAT YOU ARE INSTEAD
OF ALL THAT YOU ARE NOT

-- TINY BUDDHA

HOW MUCH SLEEP DID I GET LAST NIGHT? ....

i am so grateful...

3 THINGS I AM GRATEFUL FOR TODAY

1. ....
2. ....
3. ....

what do i love about myself...

....

....

....

....

today's priorities...

3 MOST IMPORTANT THINGS TO DO TODAY:

1. ....
2. ....
3. ....

TODAY I AM THRIVING

evening check in

movement

HOW DID I MOVE TODAY? _____

WEIGHTS❑ HIIT WORKOUT❑ ENJOYED NATURE❑ OTHER❑

HOW WAS MY ENERGY LEVEL TODAY? _____

_____

_____

_____

_____

fuel

❑ PROTEIN WITH EACH MEAL
❑ COLOR WITH EACH MEAL
WHAT COLORS DID I EAT TODAY? _____
WATER INTAKE.. HOW MANY OUNCES DID I DRINK TODAY? _____
❑ GAVE MY BODY A FOOD REST BEFORE BED SO IT IS ABLE TO FOCUS
ON RESTORING AND REPAIRING WHILE I SLEEP

reflection

WAS THIS A REALLY GOOD DAY? WHAT DID I LOVE ABOUT
TODAY? WHAT DO I WANT TO BE BETTER WITH TOMORROW?

_____

_____

_____

_____

TODAY I AM THRIVING

date _____

IF IT IS OUT OF YOUR HANDS, IT DESERVES TO BE OUT OF YOUR MIND TOO

- IVAN NURN

HOW MUCH SLEEP DID I GET LAST NIGHT? _____

i am so grateful...

3 THINGS I AM GRATEFUL FOR TODAY

1. _____
2. _____
3. _____

is there anything i need to let go of...

_____

_____

_____

_____

today's priorities...

3 MOST IMPORTANT THINGS TO DO TODAY:

1. _____
2. _____
3. _____

TODAY I AM THRIVING

evening check in

movement

HOW DID I MOVE TODAY? _____

WEIGHTS❑ HIIT WORKOUT❑ ENJOYED NATURE❑ OTHER❑

HOW WAS MY ENERGY LEVEL TODAY? _____

_____
_____
_____
_____

fuel

❑ PROTEIN WITH EACH MEAL
❑ COLOR WITH EACH MEAL
WHAT COLORS DID I EAT TODAY? _____
WATER INTAKE.. HOW MANY OUNCES DID I DRINK TODAY? _____
❑ GAVE MY BODY A FOOD REST BEFORE BED SO IT IS ABLE TO FOCUS
ON RESTORING AND REPAIRING WHILE I SLEEP

reflection

WAS THIS A REALLY GOOD DAY? WHAT DID I LOVE ABOUT
TODAY? WHAT DO I WANT TO BE BETTER WITH TOMORROW?

_____
_____
_____
_____

TODAY I AM THRIVING

date ————————————————————————

LIFE IS GOOD WHEN YOU SPEND IT WITH PEOPLE WHO MAKE YOUR HEART HAPPY

- UNKNOWN

HOW MUCH SLEEP DID I GET LAST NIGHT?

i am so grateful...

3 THINGS I AM GRATEFUL FOR TODAY

1. ....
2. ....
3. ....

who do i want to start spending more time with...

....

....

....

....

today's priorities...

3 MOST IMPORTANT THINGS TO DO TODAY:

1. ....
2. ....
3. ....

evening check in

movement

HOW DID I MOVE TODAY? ....

  WEIGHTS❑ HIIT WORKOUT❑ ENJOYED NATURE❑ OTHER❑

HOW WAS MY ENERGY LEVEL TODAY? ....

....
....
....
....

fuel

  ❑ PROTEIN WITH EACH MEAL
  ❑ COLOR WITH EACH MEAL
  WHAT COLORS DID I EAT TODAY? _____
  WATER INTAKE.. HOW MANY OUNCES DID I DRINK TODAY? _____
  ❑ GAVE MY BODY A FOOD REST BEFORE BED SO IT IS ABLE TO FOCUS
  ON RESTORING AND REPAIRING WHILE I SLEEP

reflection

  WAS THIS A REALLY GOOD DAY? WHAT DID I LOVE ABOUT
  TODAY? WHAT DO I WANT TO BE BETTER WITH TOMORROW?

....
....
....
....

TODAY I AM THRIVING

date _____

YOU WILL NEVER BE READY. JUST START
- UNKNOWN

HOW MUCH SLEEP DID I GET LAST NIGHT? _____

i am so grateful...
3 THINGS I AM GRATEFUL FOR TODAY

1. _____
2. _____
3. _____

what is something i really want to start doing...

_____

_____

_____

_____

today's priorities...
3 MOST IMPORTANT THINGS TO DO TODAY:

1. _____
2. _____
3. _____

evening check in

movement

HOW DID I MOVE TODAY? ....

WEIGHTS❑ HIIT WORKOUT❑ ENJOYED NATURE❑ OTHER❑

HOW WAS MY ENERGY LEVEL TODAY? _____

----

fuel

❑ PROTEIN WITH EACH MEAL
❑ COLOR WITH EACH MEAL
WHAT COLORS DID I EAT TODAY? _____
WATER INTAKE.. HOW MANY OUNCES DID I DRINK TODAY? _____
❑ GAVE MY BODY A FOOD REST BEFORE BED SO IT IS ABLE TO FOCUS
ON RESTORING AND REPAIRING WHILE I SLEEP

reflection

WAS THIS A REALLY GOOD DAY? WHAT DID I LOVE ABOUT
TODAY? WHAT DO I WANT TO BE BETTER WITH TOMORROW?

TODAY I AM THRIVING

date _____

INVEST IN YOURSELF. IT PAYS
THE BEST INTEREST

- UNKNOWN

HOW MUCH SLEEP DID I GET LAST NIGHT?_____

i am so grateful...

3 THINGS I AM GRATEFUL FOR TODAY

1. _____
2. _____
3. _____

what is one new thing i can do today that would make me feel good...

_____

_____

_____

_____

today's priorities...

3 MOST IMPORTANT THINGS TO DO TODAY:

1. _____
2. _____
3. _____

TODAY I AM THRIVING

evening check in

movement

HOW DID I MOVE TODAY? _____

WEIGHTS❑ HIIT WORKOUT❑ ENJOYED NATURE❑ OTHER❑

HOW WAS MY ENERGY LEVEL TODAY? _____

_____
_____
_____
_____

fuel

❑ PROTEIN WITH EACH MEAL
❑ COLOR WITH EACH MEAL
WHAT COLORS DID I EAT TODAY? _____
WATER INTAKE.. HOW MANY OUNCES DID I DRINK TODAY? _____
❑ GAVE MY BODY A FOOD REST BEFORE BED SO IT IS ABLE TO FOCUS
ON RESTORING AND REPAIRING WHILE I SLEEP

reflection

WAS THIS A REALLY GOOD DAY? WHAT DID I LOVE ABOUT
TODAY? WHAT DO I WANT TO BE BETTER WITH TOMORROW?

_____
_____
_____
_____

TODAY I AM THRIVING

weekly reflection

HOW MANY REALLY GOOD DAYS DID I HAVE THIS WEEK? WHAT DO I WANT TO WORK ON NEXT WEEK?

date _____

EXERCISE IS A CELEBRATION OF
WHAT YOUR BODY CAN DO

- UNKNOWN

HOW MUCH SLEEP DID I GET LAST NIGHT? _____

i am so grateful...

3 THINGS I AM GRATEFUL FOR TODAY

1. _____
2. _____
3. _____

a really good day today would include...

_____

_____

_____

today's priorities...

3 MOST IMPORTANT THINGS TO DO TODAY:

1. _____
2. _____
3. _____

evening check in

movement

HOW DID I MOVE TODAY? ....

WEIGHTS❑ HIIT WORKOUT❑ ENJOYED NATURE❑ OTHER❑

HOW WAS MY ENERGY LEVEL TODAY? ....

....

....

....

....

fuel

❑ PROTEIN WITH EACH MEAL
❑ COLOR WITH EACH MEAL
WHAT COLORS DID I EAT TODAY? ....
WATER INTAKE.. HOW MANY OUNCES DID I DRINK TODAY? ....
❑ GAVE MY BODY A FOOD REST BEFORE BED SO IT IS ABLE TO FOCUS
ON RESTORING AND REPAIRING WHILE I SLEEP

reflection

WAS THIS A REALLY GOOD DAY? WHAT DID I LOVE ABOUT
TODAY? WHAT DO I WANT TO BE BETTER WITH TOMORROW?

....

....

....

....

TODAY I AM THRIVING

date _____

LIVE FOR MOMENTS YOU
CAN'T PUT INTO WORDS

- CLO MAILEN

HOW MUCH SLEEP DID I GET LAST NIGHT? _____

i am so grateful...
3 THINGS I AM GRATEFUL FOR TODAY

1. _____
2. _____
3. _____

what is something i want to do that i have never done before...

_____

_____

_____

today's priorities...
3 MOST IMPORTANT THINGS TO DO TODAY:

1. _____
2. _____
3. _____

TODAY I AM THRIVING

evening check in

movement

HOW DID I MOVE TODAY? _____

    WEIGHTS❑ HIIT WORKOUT❑ ENJOYED NATURE❑ OTHER❑

HOW WAS MY ENERGY LEVEL TODAY? _____

_____

_____

_____

_____

fuel

❑ PROTEIN WITH EACH MEAL
❑ COLOR WITH EACH MEAL
WHAT COLORS DID I EAT TODAY? _____
WATER INTAKE.. HOW MANY OUNCES DID I DRINK TODAY? _____
❑ GAVE MY BODY A FOOD REST BEFORE BED SO IT IS ABLE TO FOCUS
ON RESTORING AND REPAIRING WHILE I SLEEP

reflection

    WAS THIS A REALLY GOOD DAY? WHAT DID I LOVE ABOUT
TODAY? WHAT DO I WANT TO BE BETTER WITH TOMORROW?

_____

_____

_____

_____

TODAY I AM THRIVING

date _____

DON'T BELIEVE EVERYTHING YOU THINK
- ROBERT FULGHURN

HOW MUCH SLEEP DID I GET LAST NIGHT? _____

i am so grateful...
3 THINGS I AM GRATEFUL FOR TODAY

1. _____
2. _____
3. _____

are there any negative thoughts i need to work on getting rid of...

_____

_____

_____

_____

today's priorities...
3 MOST IMPORTANT THINGS TO DO TODAY:

1. _____
2. _____
3. _____

evening check in

movement

HOW DID I MOVE TODAY? ....

WEIGHTS❏ HIIT WORKOUT❏ ENJOYED NATURE❏ OTHER❏

HOW WAS MY ENERGY LEVEL TODAY? ....

....
....
....
....

fuel

❏ PROTEIN WITH EACH MEAL
❏ COLOR WITH EACH MEAL
WHAT COLORS DID I EAT TODAY? ....
WATER INTAKE.. HOW MANY OUNCES DID I DRINK TODAY? ....
❏ GAVE MY BODY A FOOD REST BEFORE BED SO IT IS ABLE TO FOCUS
ON RESTORING AND REPAIRING WHILE I SLEEP

reflection

WAS THIS A REALLY GOOD DAY? WHAT DID I LOVE ABOUT
TODAY? WHAT DO I WANT TO BE BETTER WITH TOMORROW?

....
....
....

TODAY I AM THRIVING

date ——————————————————————

THIS IS YOUR REMINDER THAT YOUR BODY IS THE ONLY ONE YOU HAVE. TREAT IT WELL

- UNKNOWN

HOW MUCH SLEEP DID I GET LAST NIGHT? ....

i am so grateful...

3 THINGS I AM GRATEFUL FOR TODAY

1. ....
2. ....
3. ....

how well am i treating my body...

....
....
....
....

today's priorities...

3 MOST IMPORTANT THINGS TO DO TODAY:

1. ....
2. ....
3. ....

TODAY I AM THRIVING

evening check in

movement

HOW DID I MOVE TODAY? ....

    WEIGHTS❑ HIIT WORKOUT❑ ENJOYED NATURE❑ OTHER❑

HOW WAS MY ENERGY LEVEL TODAY? ....

....
....
....
....

fuel

❑ PROTEIN WITH EACH MEAL
❑ COLOR WITH EACH MEAL
WHAT COLORS DID I EAT TODAY? ....
WATER INTAKE.. HOW MANY OUNCES DID I DRINK TODAY? ....
❑ GAVE MY BODY A FOOD REST BEFORE BED SO IT IS ABLE TO FOCUS
ON RESTORING AND REPAIRING WHILE I SLEEP

reflection

    WAS THIS A REALLY GOOD DAY? WHAT DID I LOVE ABOUT
TODAY? WHAT DO I WANT TO BE BETTER WITH TOMORROW?

....
....
....
....

TODAY I AM THRIVING

date ———————————————————————

IF YOU GET TIRED, LEARN
TO REST NOT QUIT

- BANKSY

HOW MUCH SLEEP DID I GET LAST NIGHT? ——————————————

i am so grateful...

3 THINGS I AM GRATEFUL FOR TODAY

1. ——————————————————————————
2. ——————————————————————————
3. ——————————————————————————

is there anything i need to do to increase my energy...

———————————————————————————————

———————————————————————————————

———————————————————————————————

———————————————————————————————

today's priorities...

3 MOST IMPORTANT THINGS TO DO TODAY:

1. ——————————————————————————
2. ——————————————————————————
3. ——————————————————————————

evening check in

movement

HOW DID I MOVE TODAY? _____

WEIGHTS❏ HIIT WORKOUT❏ ENJOYED NATURE❏ OTHER❏

HOW WAS MY ENERGY LEVEL TODAY? _____

_____
_____
_____
_____

fuel

❏ PROTEIN WITH EACH MEAL
❏ COLOR WITH EACH MEAL
WHAT COLORS DID I EAT TODAY? _____
WATER INTAKE.. HOW MANY OUNCES DID I DRINK TODAY? _____
❏ GAVE MY BODY A FOOD REST BEFORE BED SO IT IS ABLE TO FOCUS
ON RESTORING AND REPAIRING WHILE I SLEEP

reflection

WAS THIS A REALLY GOOD DAY? WHAT DID I LOVE ABOUT
TODAY? WHAT DO I WANT TO BE BETTER WITH TOMORROW?

_____
_____
_____
_____

date _____

THE BEST WAY TO GET THINGS
DONE IS TO BEGIN

- UNKNOWN

HOW MUCH SLEEP DID I GET LAST NIGHT?_____

i am so grateful...

3 THINGS I AM GRATEFUL FOR TODAY

1. _____
2. _____
3. _____

what do i want to focus on starting...

_____
_____
_____
_____

today's priorities...

3 MOST IMPORTANT THINGS TO DO TODAY:

1. _____
2. _____
3. _____

evening check in

movement

HOW DID I MOVE TODAY? _____

WEIGHTS❑ HIIT WORKOUT❑ ENJOYED NATURE❑ OTHER❑

HOW WAS MY ENERGY LEVEL TODAY? _____

_____
_____
_____
_____

fuel

❑ PROTEIN WITH EACH MEAL
❑ COLOR WITH EACH MEAL
WHAT COLORS DID I EAT TODAY? _____
WATER INTAKE.. HOW MANY OUNCES DID I DRINK TODAY? _____
❑ GAVE MY BODY A FOOD REST BEFORE BED SO IT IS ABLE TO FOCUS
ON RESTORING AND REPAIRING WHILE I SLEEP

reflection

WAS THIS A REALLY GOOD DAY? WHAT DID I LOVE ABOUT
TODAY? WHAT DO I WANT TO BE BETTER WITH TOMORROW?

_____
_____
_____
_____

TODAY I AM THRIVING

date —————————————————————————

BUILD GOOD HABITS THAT
WILL CHANGE YOUR LIFE

- UNKNOWN

HOW MUCH SLEEP DID I GET LAST NIGHT?_____

i am so grateful...

3 THINGS I AM GRATEFUL FOR TODAY

1. _____
2. _____
3. _____

what are my good daily habits...

_____
_____
_____
_____

today's priorities...

3 MOST IMPORTANT THINGS TO DO TODAY:

1. _____
2. _____
3. _____

evening check in

movement

HOW DID I MOVE TODAY? ....

    WEIGHTS❑ HIIT WORKOUT❑ ENJOYED NATURE❑ OTHER❑

HOW WAS MY ENERGY LEVEL TODAY? ....

....
....
....
....

fuel

❑ PROTEIN WITH EACH MEAL
❑ COLOR WITH EACH MEAL
WHAT COLORS DID I EAT TODAY? ....
WATER INTAKE.. HOW MANY OUNCES DID I DRINK TODAY? ....
❑ GAVE MY BODY A FOOD REST BEFORE BED SO IT IS ABLE TO FOCUS
ON RESTORING AND REPAIRING WHILE I SLEEP

reflection

    WAS THIS A REALLY GOOD DAY? WHAT DID I LOVE ABOUT
TODAY? WHAT DO I WANT TO BE BETTER WITH TOMORROW?

....
....
....
....

TODAY I AM THRIVING

weekly reflection

HOW MANY REALLY GOOD DAYS DID I HAVE THIS WEEK? WHAT DO I WANT TO WORK ON NEXT WEEK?

_____

_____

_____

_____

_____

_____

_____

_____

_____

_____

_____

_____

_____

_____

_____

date _____

YOUR BODY IS A REFLECTION
OF YOUR LIFESTYLE

- UNKNOWN

HOW MUCH SLEEP DID I GET LAST NIGHT?_____

i am so grateful...

3 THINGS I AM GRATEFUL FOR TODAY

1. _____
2. _____
3. _____

what parts of my lifestyle are creating better health...

_____

_____

_____

today's priorities...

3 MOST IMPORTANT THINGS TO DO TODAY:

1. _____
2. _____
3. _____

evening check in

movement

HOW DID I MOVE TODAY? _____

    WEIGHTS❑ HIIT WORKOUT❑ ENJOYED NATURE❑ OTHER❑

HOW WAS MY ENERGY LEVEL TODAY? _____

_____

_____

_____

_____

fuel

❑ PROTEIN WITH EACH MEAL
❑ COLOR WITH EACH MEAL
WHAT COLORS DID I EAT TODAY? _____
WATER INTAKE.. HOW MANY OUNCES DID I DRINK TODAY? _____
❑ GAVE MY BODY A FOOD REST BEFORE BED SO IT IS ABLE TO FOCUS
ON RESTORING AND REPAIRING WHILE I SLEEP

reflection

    WAS THIS A REALLY GOOD DAY? WHAT DID I LOVE ABOUT
TODAY? WHAT DO I WANT TO BE BETTER WITH TOMORROW?

_____

_____

_____

_____

TODAY I AM THRIVING

date _____

NEVER LOOK BACK UNLESS YOU ARE
SEEING HOW FAR YOU HAVE COME

- UNKNOWN

HOW MUCH SLEEP DID I GET LAST NIGHT?_____

i am so grateful...

3 THINGS I AM GRATEFUL FOR TODAY

1. _____
2. _____
3. _____

what are some things you are most proud of...

_____

_____

_____

_____

today's priorities...

3 MOST IMPORTANT THINGS TO DO TODAY:

1. _____
2. _____
3. _____

TODAY I AM THRIVING

evening check in

movement

HOW DID I MOVE TODAY? _____

WEIGHTS❑ HIIT WORKOUT❑ ENJOYED NATURE❑ OTHER❑

HOW WAS MY ENERGY LEVEL TODAY? _____

_____
_____
_____
_____

fuel

❑ PROTEIN WITH EACH MEAL
❑ COLOR WITH EACH MEAL
WHAT COLORS DID I EAT TODAY? _____
WATER INTAKE.. HOW MANY OUNCES DID I DRINK TODAY? _____
❑ GAVE MY BODY A FOOD REST BEFORE BED SO IT IS ABLE TO FOCUS
ON RESTORING AND REPAIRING WHILE I SLEEP

reflection

WAS THIS A REALLY GOOD DAY? WHAT DID I LOVE ABOUT
TODAY? WHAT DO I WANT TO BE BETTER WITH TOMORROW?

_____
_____
_____
_____

TODAY I AM THRIVING

date _____

THE GREATEST GIFT YOU CAN
GIVE YOUR FAMILY AND THE
WORLD IS A HEALTHY YOU

– JOYCE MEYER

HOW MUCH SLEEP DID I GET LAST NIGHT? ....

i am so grateful...

3 THINGS I AM GRATEFUL FOR TODAY

1. ....
2. ....
3. ....

is there anything i want to work on with my health...

....

....

....

....

today's priorities...

3 MOST IMPORTANT THINGS TO DO TODAY:

1. ....
2. ....
3. ....

TODAY I AM THRIVING

evening check in

movement

HOW DID I MOVE TODAY? ....

    WEIGHTS❑ HIIT WORKOUT❑ ENJOYED NATURE❑ OTHER❑

HOW WAS MY ENERGY LEVEL TODAY? ....

....
....
....
....

fuel

❑ PROTEIN WITH EACH MEAL
❑ COLOR WITH EACH MEAL
WHAT COLORS DID I EAT TODAY? _____
WATER INTAKE.. HOW MANY OUNCES DID I DRINK TODAY? _____
❑ GAVE MY BODY A FOOD REST BEFORE BED SO IT IS ABLE TO FOCUS
ON RESTORING AND REPAIRING WHILE I SLEEP

reflection

    WAS THIS A REALLY GOOD DAY? WHAT DID I LOVE ABOUT
    TODAY? WHAT DO I WANT TO BE BETTER WITH TOMORROW?

....
....
....
....

TODAY I AM THRIVING

date _____

ALMOST EVERYTHING WILL WORK AGAIN IF YOU UNPLUG IT FOR A FEW MINUTES. INCLUDING YOU

- ANNE LAMOTT

HOW MUCH SLEEP DID I GET LAST NIGHT? ....

i am so grateful...

3 THINGS I AM GRATEFUL FOR TODAY

1. ....
2. ....
3. ....

what self care do you need today...

....

....

....

....

today's priorities...

3 MOST IMPORTANT THINGS TO DO TODAY:

1. ....
2. ....
3. ....

evening check in

movement

HOW DID I MOVE TODAY? ....

WEIGHTS❑ HIIT WORKOUT❑ ENJOYED NATURE❑ OTHER❑

HOW WAS MY ENERGY LEVEL TODAY? ....

....

....

....

....

fuel

❑ PROTEIN WITH EACH MEAL
❑ COLOR WITH EACH MEAL
WHAT COLORS DID I EAT TODAY? ....
WATER INTAKE.. HOW MANY OUNCES DID I DRINK TODAY? ....
❑ GAVE MY BODY A FOOD REST BEFORE BED SO IT IS ABLE TO FOCUS
ON RESTORING AND REPAIRING WHILE I SLEEP

reflection

WAS THIS A REALLY GOOD DAY? WHAT DID I LOVE ABOUT
TODAY? WHAT DO I WANT TO BE BETTER WITH TOMORROW?

....

....

....

....

TODAY I AM THRIVING

date _____

HAVING A HEALTHY MIND IS JUST AS IMPORTANT AS HAVING A HEALTHY BODY

- UNKNOWN

HOW MUCH SLEEP DID I GET LAST NIGHT? _____

i am so grateful...

3 THINGS I AM GRATEFUL FOR TODAY

1. ....
2. ....
3. ....

what inspires me...

....
....
....
....

today's priorities...

3 MOST IMPORTANT THINGS TO DO TODAY:

1. ....
2. ....
3. ....

evening check in

movement

HOW DID I MOVE TODAY? _____

WEIGHTS❑ HIIT WORKOUT❑ ENJOYED NATURE❑ OTHER❑

HOW WAS MY ENERGY LEVEL TODAY? _____

_____

_____

_____

_____

fuel

❑ PROTEIN WITH EACH MEAL
❑ COLOR WITH EACH MEAL
WHAT COLORS DID I EAT TODAY? _____
WATER INTAKE.. HOW MANY OUNCES DID I DRINK TODAY? _____
❑ GAVE MY BODY A FOOD REST BEFORE BED SO IT IS ABLE TO FOCUS
ON RESTORING AND REPAIRING WHILE I SLEEP

reflection

WAS THIS A REALLY GOOD DAY? WHAT DID I LOVE ABOUT
TODAY? WHAT DO I WANT TO BE BETTER WITH TOMORROW?

_____

_____

_____

_____

TODAY I AM THRIVING

date _____

THE BEST TIME FOR NEW
BEGINNINGS IS NOW

- UNKNOWN

HOW MUCH SLEEP DID I GET LAST NIGHT?_____

i am so grateful...

3 THINGS I AM GRATEFUL FOR TODAY

1. _____
2. _____
3. _____

what is one new thing i want to work on...

_____
_____
_____
_____

today's priorities...

3 MOST IMPORTANT THINGS TO DO TODAY:

1. _____
2. _____
3. _____

TODAY I AM THRIVING

evening check in

movement

HOW DID I MOVE TODAY? ....

WEIGHTS❑ HIIT WORKOUT❑ ENJOYED NATURE❑ OTHER❑

HOW WAS MY ENERGY LEVEL TODAY? ....

....

....

....

....

fuel

❑ PROTEIN WITH EACH MEAL
❑ COLOR WITH EACH MEAL
WHAT COLORS DID I EAT TODAY? ....
WATER INTAKE.. HOW MANY OUNCES DID I DRINK TODAY? ....
❑ GAVE MY BODY A FOOD REST BEFORE BED SO IT IS ABLE TO FOCUS
ON RESTORING AND REPAIRING WHILE I SLEEP

reflection

WAS THIS A REALLY GOOD DAY? WHAT DID I LOVE ABOUT
TODAY? WHAT DO I WANT TO BE BETTER WITH TOMORROW?

....

....

....

....

TODAY I AM THRIVING

date _____

YOU CAN'T CHANGE THE PEOPLE AROUND YOU. BUT YOU CAN CHANGE WHO YOU CHOOSE TO BE AROUND

- UNKNOWN

HOW MUCH SLEEP DID I GET LAST NIGHT? ....

i am so grateful...

3 THINGS I AM GRATEFUL FOR TODAY

1. _____
2. _____
3. _____

what are some of your favorite qualities in people...

_____
_____
_____
_____

today's priorities...

3 MOST IMPORTANT THINGS TO DO TODAY:

1. _____
2. _____
3. _____

TODAY I AM THRIVING

evening check in

movement

HOW DID I MOVE TODAY? _____

    WEIGHTS❑ HIIT WORKOUT❑ ENJOYED NATURE❑ OTHER❑

HOW WAS MY ENERGY LEVEL TODAY? _____

_____

_____

_____

_____

fuel

❑ PROTEIN WITH EACH MEAL
❑ COLOR WITH EACH MEAL
WHAT COLORS DID I EAT TODAY? _____
WATER INTAKE.. HOW MANY OUNCES DID I DRINK TODAY? _____
❑ GAVE MY BODY A FOOD REST BEFORE BED SO IT IS ABLE TO FOCUS
ON RESTORING AND REPAIRING WHILE I SLEEP

reflection

    WAS THIS A REALLY GOOD DAY? WHAT DID I LOVE ABOUT
    TODAY? WHAT DO I WANT TO BE BETTER WITH TOMORROW?

_____

_____

_____

_____

weekly reflection

HOW MANY REALLY GOOD DAYS DID I HAVE THIS WEEK? WHAT DO I WANT TO WORK ON NEXT WEEK?

date _____

SAY YES TO NEW ADVENTURES

- UNKNOWN

HOW MUCH SLEEP DID I GET LAST NIGHT? _____

i am so grateful...

3 THINGS I AM GRATEFUL FOR TODAY

1. _____
2. _____
3. _____

what are some new things i can do this week...

_____
_____
_____
_____

today's priorities...

3 MOST IMPORTANT THINGS TO DO TODAY:

1. _____
2. _____
3. _____

evening check in ———————————————————

movement

HOW DID I MOVE TODAY? _____

WEIGHTS❑ HIIT WORKOUT❑ ENJOYED NATURE❑ OTHER❑

HOW WAS MY ENERGY LEVEL TODAY? _____

_____
_____
_____
_____

fuel

❑ PROTEIN WITH EACH MEAL
❑ COLOR WITH EACH MEAL
WHAT COLORS DID I EAT TODAY? _____
WATER INTAKE.. HOW MANY OUNCES DID I DRINK TODAY? _____
❑ GAVE MY BODY A FOOD REST BEFORE BED SO IT IS ABLE TO FOCUS
ON RESTORING AND REPAIRING WHILE I SLEEP

reflection

WAS THIS A REALLY GOOD DAY? WHAT DID I LOVE ABOUT
TODAY? WHAT DO I WANT TO BE BETTER WITH TOMORROW?

_____
_____
_____
_____

TODAY I AM THRIVING

date ————————————————————

THE SECRET OF YOUR FUTURE IS
HIDDEN IN YOUR DAILY ROUTINE

- MIKE MURDOCK

HOW MUCH SLEEP DID I GET LAST NIGHT?

i am so grateful...

3 THINGS I AM GRATEFUL FOR TODAY

1. _____
2. _____
3. _____

what are some daily habits i would like to incorporate...

_____
_____
_____
_____

today's priorities...

3 MOST IMPORTANT THINGS TO DO TODAY:

1. _____
2. _____
3. _____

---

evening check in ————————————————

movement

HOW DID I MOVE TODAY? ....

     WEIGHTS❑ HIIT WORKOUT❑ ENJOYED NATURE❑ OTHER❑

HOW WAS MY ENERGY LEVEL TODAY? ....

....
....
....
....

fuel

❑ PROTEIN WITH EACH MEAL
❑ COLOR WITH EACH MEAL
WHAT COLORS DID I EAT TODAY? ....
WATER INTAKE.. HOW MANY OUNCES DID I DRINK TODAY? ....
❑ GAVE MY BODY A FOOD REST BEFORE BED SO IT IS ABLE TO FOCUS
ON RESTORING AND REPAIRING WHILE I SLEEP

reflection

     WAS THIS A REALLY GOOD DAY? WHAT DID I LOVE ABOUT
TODAY? WHAT DO I WANT TO BE BETTER WITH TOMORROW?

....
....
....
....

TODAY I AM THRIVING

date _____

BE THE PERSON YOU WANT
TO HAVE IN YOUR LIFE

- UNKNOWN

HOW MUCH SLEEP DID I GET LAST NIGHT? _____

i am so grateful...

3 THINGS I AM GRATEFUL FOR TODAY

1. _____
2. _____
3. _____

what are some qualities you want to work on?

_____

_____

_____

_____

today's priorities...

3 MOST IMPORTANT THINGS TO DO TODAY:

1. _____
2. _____
3. _____

TODAY I AM THRIVING

evening check in

movement

HOW DID I MOVE TODAY? ....

WEIGHTS❑ HIIT WORKOUT❑ ENJOYED NATURE❑ OTHER❑

HOW WAS MY ENERGY LEVEL TODAY? ....

....
....
....
....

fuel

❑ PROTEIN WITH EACH MEAL
❑ COLOR WITH EACH MEAL
WHAT COLORS DID I EAT TODAY? ....
WATER INTAKE.. HOW MANY OUNCES DID I DRINK TODAY? ....
❑ GAVE MY BODY A FOOD REST BEFORE BED SO IT IS ABLE TO FOCUS
ON RESTORING AND REPAIRING WHILE I SLEEP

reflection

WAS THIS A REALLY GOOD DAY? WHAT DID I LOVE ABOUT
TODAY? WHAT DO I WANT TO BE BETTER WITH TOMORROW?

....
....
....
....

TODAY I AM THRIVING

date _____

INVEST IN YOUR MIND. INVEST IN YOUR HEALTH. INVEST IN YOURSELF

- UNKNOWN

HOW MUCH SLEEP DID I GET LAST NIGHT? _____

i am so grateful...

3 THINGS I AM GRATEFUL FOR TODAY

1. _____
2. _____
3. _____

what area of my health do i want to focus on most today...

_____
_____
_____
_____

TODAY'S PRIORITIES... 3 MOST IMPORATN THINGS TO DO TODAY:

1. _____
2. _____
3. _____

evening check in

movement

HOW DID I MOVE TODAY? ....

WEIGHTS❑ HIIT WORKOUT❑ ENJOYED NATURE❑ OTHER❑

HOW WAS MY ENERGY LEVEL TODAY? ....

....

....

....

....

fuel

❑ PROTEIN WITH EACH MEAL
❑ COLOR WITH EACH MEAL
WHAT COLORS DID I EAT TODAY? ....
WATER INTAKE.. HOW MANY OUNCES DID I DRINK TODAY? ....
❑ GAVE MY BODY A FOOD REST BEFORE BED SO IT IS ABLE TO FOCUS
ON RESTORING AND REPAIRING WHILE I SLEEP

reflection

WAS THIS A REALLY GOOD DAY? WHAT DID I LOVE ABOUT
TODAY? WHAT DO I WANT TO BE BETTER WITH TOMORROW?

....

....

....

....

TODAY I AM THRIVING

date _____

DAILY REMINDER… KEEP
GOING. KEEP GROWING

- UNKNOWN

HOW MUCH SLEEP DID I GET LAST NIGHT? _____

i am so grateful...

3 THINGS I AM GRATEFUL FOR TODAY

1. _____
2. _____
3. _____

what area do i want to focus on growing in...

_____
_____
_____
_____

today's priorities...

3 MOST IMPORTANT THINGS TO DO TODAY:

1. _____
2. _____
3. _____

evening check in

movement

HOW DID I MOVE TODAY? ....

WEIGHTS❑ HIIT WORKOUT❑ ENJOYED NATURE❑ OTHER❑

HOW WAS MY ENERGY LEVEL TODAY? ....

....
....
....
....

fuel

❑ PROTEIN WITH EACH MEAL
❑ COLOR WITH EACH MEAL
WHAT COLORS DID I EAT TODAY? ....
WATER INTAKE.. HOW MANY OUNCES DID I DRINK TODAY? ....
❑ GAVE MY BODY A FOOD REST BEFORE BED SO IT IS ABLE TO FOCUS
ON RESTORING AND REPAIRING WHILE I SLEEP

reflection

WAS THIS A REALLY GOOD DAY? WHAT DID I LOVE ABOUT
TODAY? WHAT DO I WANT TO BE BETTER WITH TOMORROW?

....
....
....
....

date —————————————————

IT'S NEVER TOO EARLY OR TOO LATE TO WORK TOWARDS BEING THE HEALTHIEST YOU

- UNKNOWN

HOW MUCH SLEEP DID I GET LAST NIGHT? ....

i am so grateful...

3 THINGS I AM GRATEFUL FOR TODAY

1. ....
2. ....
3. ....

i feel healthy when...

....
....
....
....

today's priorities...

3 MOST IMPORTANT THINGS TO DO TODAY:

1. ....
2. ....
3. ....

evening check in

movement

HOW DID I MOVE TODAY? ....

WEIGHTS☐ HIIT WORKOUT☐ ENJOYED NATURE☐ OTHER☐

HOW WAS MY ENERGY LEVEL TODAY? ....

....
....
....
....

fuel

☐ PROTEIN WITH EACH MEAL
☐ COLOR WITH EACH MEAL
WHAT COLORS DID I EAT TODAY? ....
WATER INTAKE.. HOW MANY OUNCES DID I DRINK TODAY? ....
☐ GAVE MY BODY A FOOD REST BEFORE BED SO IT IS ABLE TO FOCUS
ON RESTORING AND REPAIRING WHILE I SLEEP

reflection

WAS THIS A REALLY GOOD DAY? WHAT DID I LOVE ABOUT
TODAY? WHAT DO I WANT TO BE BETTER WITH TOMORROW?

....
....
....
....

date _____

YOU WILL NEVER START YOUR NEXT CHAPTER IF YOU KEEP RE-READING THIS ONE

— UNKNOWN

HOW MUCH SLEEP DID I GET LAST NIGHT? _____

i am so grateful...

3 THINGS I AM GRATEFUL FOR TODAY

1. _____
2. _____
3. _____

what do i want my next chapter to look like...

_____
_____
_____
_____

today's priorities...

3 MOST IMPORTANT THINGS TO DO TODAY:

1. _____
2. _____
3. _____

TODAY I AM THRIVING

evening check in

movement

HOW DID I MOVE TODAY? ....

WEIGHTS❑ HIIT WORKOUT❑ ENJOYED NATURE❑ OTHER❑

HOW WAS MY ENERGY LEVEL TODAY? ....

....

....

....

....

fuel

❑ PROTEIN WITH EACH MEAL
❑ COLOR WITH EACH MEAL
WHAT COLORS DID I EAT TODAY? ....
WATER INTAKE.. HOW MANY OUNCES DID I DRINK TODAY? ....
❑ GAVE MY BODY A FOOD REST BEFORE BED SO IT IS ABLE TO FOCUS
ON RESTORING AND REPAIRING WHILE I SLEEP

reflection

WAS THIS A REALLY GOOD DAY? WHAT DID I LOVE ABOUT
TODAY? WHAT DO I WANT TO BE BETTER WITH TOMORROW?

....

....

....

....

TODAY I AM THRIVING

weekly reflection

HOW MANY REALLY GOOD DAYS DID I HAVE THIS WEEK? WHAT DO I WANT TO WORK ON NEXT WEEK?

_____

_____

_____

_____

_____

_____

_____

_____

_____

_____

_____

_____

_____

_____

date ―――――――――――――――――――――

WHAT IF EVERYTHING YOU ARE
GOING THROUGH IS PREPARING
YOU FOR WHAT YOU ASKED FOR

- SIRI LUNDLEY

HOW MUCH SLEEP DID I GET LAST NIGHT? ....

i am so grateful...

3 THINGS I AM GRATEFUL FOR TODAY

1. ....
2. ....
3. ....

what are some things you are working on creating...

....
....
....
....

today's priorities...

3 MOST IMPORTANT THINGS TO DO TODAY:

1. ....
2. ....
3. ....

evening check in

movement

HOW DID I MOVE TODAY? ....

WEIGHTS❏ HIIT WORKOUT❏ ENJOYED NATURE❏ OTHER❏

HOW WAS MY ENERGY LEVEL TODAY? ....

....
....
....
....

fuel

❏ PROTEIN WITH EACH MEAL
❏ COLOR WITH EACH MEAL
WHAT COLORS DID I EAT TODAY? _____
WATER INTAKE.. HOW MANY OUNCES DID I DRINK TODAY? _____
❏ GAVE MY BODY A FOOD REST BEFORE BED SO IT IS ABLE TO FOCUS
ON RESTORING AND REPAIRING WHILE I SLEEP

reflection

WAS THIS A REALLY GOOD DAY? WHAT DID I LOVE ABOUT
TODAY? WHAT DO I WANT TO BE BETTER WITH TOMORROW?

....
....
....
....

TODAY I AM THRIVING

date _____

TREAT YOUR BODY LIKE IT BELONGS
TO SOMEONE YOU LOVE

- UNKNOWN

HOW MUCH SLEEP DID I GET LAST NIGHT?_____

i am so grateful...
3 THINGS I AM GRATEFUL FOR TODAY

1. _____
2. _____
3. _____

who in your life lifts you up...

_____
_____
_____
_____

today's priorities...
3 MOST IMPORTANT THINGS TO DO TODAY:

1. _____
2. _____
3. _____

TODAY I AM THRIVING

evening check in

movement

HOW DID I MOVE TODAY? ....

WEIGHTS❑ HIIT WORKOUT❑ ENJOYED NATURE❑ OTHER❑

HOW WAS MY ENERGY LEVEL TODAY? ....

....
....
....
....

fuel

❑ PROTEIN WITH EACH MEAL
❑ COLOR WITH EACH MEAL
WHAT COLORS DID I EAT TODAY? ....
WATER INTAKE.. HOW MANY OUNCES DID I DRINK TODAY? ....
❑ GAVE MY BODY A FOOD REST BEFORE BED SO IT IS ABLE TO FOCUS
ON RESTORING AND REPAIRING WHILE I SLEEP

reflection

WAS THIS A REALLY GOOD DAY? WHAT DID I LOVE ABOUT
TODAY? WHAT DO I WANT TO BE BETTER WITH TOMORROW?

....
....
....
....

TODAY I AM THRIVING

date _____

ALWAYS BELIEVE THAT SOMETHING WONDERFUL IS ABOUT TO HAPPEN

- UNKNOWN

HOW MUCH SLEEP DID I GET LAST NIGHT? _____

i am so grateful...

3 THINGS I AM GRATEFUL FOR TODAY

1. _____
2. _____
3. _____

i like me best when...

_____

_____

_____

_____

today's priorities...

3 MOST IMPORTANT THINGS TO DO TODAY:

1. _____
2. _____
3. _____

evening check in

movement

HOW DID I MOVE TODAY? _____

WEIGHTS❑ HIIT WORKOUT❑ ENJOYED NATURE❑ OTHER❑

HOW WAS MY ENERGY LEVEL TODAY? _____

_____
_____
_____
_____

fuel

❑ PROTEIN WITH EACH MEAL
❑ COLOR WITH EACH MEAL
WHAT COLORS DID I EAT TODAY? _____
WATER INTAKE.. HOW MANY OUNCES DID I DRINK TODAY? _____
❑ GAVE MY BODY A FOOD REST BEFORE BED SO IT IS ABLE TO FOCUS
ON RESTORING AND REPAIRING WHILE I SLEEP

reflection

WAS THIS A REALLY GOOD DAY? WHAT DID I LOVE ABOUT
TODAY? WHAT DO I WANT TO BE BETTER WITH TOMORROW?

_____
_____
_____
_____

TODAY I AM THRIVING

date _____

WHERE YOU ARE A YEAR FROM NOW
IS A REFLECTION OF THE CHOICES
YOU CHOOSE TO MAKE RIGHT NOW

- UNKNOWN

HOW MUCH SLEEP DID I GET LAST NIGHT? ....

i am so grateful...

3 THINGS I AM GRATEFUL FOR TODAY

1. ....
2. ....
3. ....

where do you see yourself a year from now...

....

....

....

....

today's priorities...

3 MOST IMPORTANT THINGS TO DO TODAY:

1. ....
2. ....
3. ....

evening check in

movement

HOW DID I MOVE TODAY? ....

WEIGHTS❑ HIIT WORKOUT❑ ENJOYED NATURE❑ OTHER❑

HOW WAS MY ENERGY LEVEL TODAY? ....

....
....
....
....

fuel

❑ PROTEIN WITH EACH MEAL
❑ COLOR WITH EACH MEAL
WHAT COLORS DID I EAT TODAY? ....
WATER INTAKE.. HOW MANY OUNCES DID I DRINK TODAY? ....
❑ GAVE MY BODY A FOOD REST BEFORE BED SO IT IS ABLE TO FOCUS
ON RESTORING AND REPAIRING WHILE I SLEEP

reflection

WAS THIS A REALLY GOOD DAY? WHAT DID I LOVE ABOUT
TODAY? WHAT DO I WANT TO BE BETTER WITH TOMORROW?

....
....
....
....

TODAY I AM THRIVING

date _____

IMAGINE WHAT IS POSSIBLE IF YOU
STOP DOUBTING YOURSELF

- UNKNOWN

HOW MUCH SLEEP DID I GET LAST NIGHT?_____

i am so grateful...

3 THINGS I AM GRATEFUL FOR TODAY

1. _____
2. _____
3. _____

what is something you are afraid to do...

_____
_____
_____
_____

today's priorities...

3 MOST IMPORTANT THINGS TO DO TODAY:

1. _____
2. _____
3. _____

TODAY I AM THRIVING

evening check in

movement

HOW DID I MOVE TODAY? ....

WEIGHTS❑ HIIT WORKOUT❑ ENJOYED NATURE❑ OTHER❑

HOW WAS MY ENERGY LEVEL TODAY? _____

....

....

....

....

fuel

❑ PROTEIN WITH EACH MEAL
❑ COLOR WITH EACH MEAL
WHAT COLORS DID I EAT TODAY? _____
WATER INTAKE.. HOW MANY OUNCES DID I DRINK TODAY? ....
❑ GAVE MY BODY A FOOD REST BEFORE BED SO IT IS ABLE TO FOCUS
ON RESTORING AND REPAIRING WHILE I SLEEP

reflection

WAS THIS A REALLY GOOD DAY? WHAT DID I LOVE ABOUT
TODAY? WHAT DO I WANT TO BE BETTER WITH TOMORROW?

....

....

....

....

TODAY I AM THRIVING

date ⸻⸻⸻⸻⸻⸻⸻⸻⸻

FALL IN LOVE WITH TAKING
CARE OF YOURSELF

- SYLVESTER MCNUTT

HOW MUCH SLEEP DID I GET LAST NIGHT? ⸻⸻⸻⸻⸻⸻

i am so grateful...

3 THINGS I AM GRATEFUL FOR TODAY

1. ⸻⸻⸻⸻⸻⸻⸻⸻⸻⸻⸻⸻
2. ⸻⸻⸻⸻⸻⸻⸻⸻⸻⸻⸻⸻
3. ⸻⸻⸻⸻⸻⸻⸻⸻⸻⸻⸻⸻

what would make me really happy today...

⸻⸻⸻⸻⸻⸻⸻⸻⸻⸻⸻⸻⸻

⸻⸻⸻⸻⸻⸻⸻⸻⸻⸻⸻⸻⸻

⸻⸻⸻⸻⸻⸻⸻⸻⸻⸻⸻⸻⸻

⸻⸻⸻⸻⸻⸻⸻⸻⸻⸻⸻⸻⸻

today's priorities...

3 MOST IMPORTANT THINGS TO DO TODAY:

1. ⸻⸻⸻⸻⸻⸻⸻⸻⸻⸻⸻⸻
2. ⸻⸻⸻⸻⸻⸻⸻⸻⸻⸻⸻⸻
3. ⸻⸻⸻⸻⸻⸻⸻⸻⸻⸻⸻⸻

evening check in

movement

HOW DID I MOVE TODAY? ....

WEIGHTS❑ HIIT WORKOUT❑ ENJOYED NATURE❑ OTHER❑

HOW WAS MY ENERGY LEVEL TODAY? _____

....

....

....

....

fuel

❑ PROTEIN WITH EACH MEAL
❑ COLOR WITH EACH MEAL
WHAT COLORS DID I EAT TODAY? _____
WATER INTAKE.. HOW MANY OUNCES DID I DRINK TODAY? _____
❑ GAVE MY BODY A FOOD REST BEFORE BED SO IT IS ABLE TO FOCUS
ON RESTORING AND REPAIRING WHILE I SLEEP

reflection

WAS THIS A REALLY GOOD DAY? WHAT DID I LOVE ABOUT
TODAY? WHAT DO I WANT TO BE BETTER WITH TOMORROW?

....

....

....

....

TODAY I AM THRIVING

date _____

GO THE EXTRA MILE. IT'S NEVER CROWDED THERE

– WAYNE DYER

HOW MUCH SLEEP DID I GET LAST NIGHT?_____

i am so grateful...

3 THINGS I AM GRATEFUL FOR TODAY

1. _____
2. _____
3. _____

what is something i want to put more effort into...

_____

_____

_____

_____

today's priorities...

3 MOST IMPORTANT THINGS TO DO TODAY:

1. _____
2. _____
3. _____

evening check in

movement

HOW DID I MOVE TODAY? ....

   WEIGHTS❑ HIIT WORKOUT❑ ENJOYED NATURE❑ OTHER❑

HOW WAS MY ENERGY LEVEL TODAY? ....

....
....
....
....

fuel

   ❑ PROTEIN WITH EACH MEAL
   ❑ COLOR WITH EACH MEAL
   WHAT COLORS DID I EAT TODAY? ....
   WATER INTAKE.. HOW MANY OUNCES DID I DRINK TODAY? ....
   ❑ GAVE MY BODY A FOOD REST BEFORE BED SO IT IS ABLE TO FOCUS
   ON RESTORING AND REPAIRING WHILE I SLEEP

reflection

   WAS THIS A REALLY GOOD DAY? WHAT DID I LOVE ABOUT
   TODAY? WHAT DO I WANT TO BE BETTER WITH TOMORROW?

....
....
....
....

TODAY I AM THRIVING

weekly reflection

HOW MANY REALLY GOOD DAYS DID I HAVE THIS WEEK? WHAT DO I WANT TO WORK ON NEXT WEEK?

date _____

IF YOU ARE ALWAYS GETTING READY
FOR THE NEXT THING, HOW WILL
YOU EVER ENJOY THIS THING

- UNKNOWN

HOW MUCH SLEEP DID I GET LAST NIGHT? _____

i am so grateful...

3 THINGS I AM GRATEFUL FOR TODAY

1. _____
2. _____
3. _____

what little things have you been taking forgranted...

_____
_____
_____
_____

today's priorities...

3 MOST IMPORTANT THINGS TO DO TODAY:

1. _____
2. _____
3. _____

evening check in

movement

HOW DID I MOVE TODAY? ....

    WEIGHTS❑ HIIT WORKOUT❑ ENJOYED NATURE❑ OTHER❑

HOW WAS MY ENERGY LEVEL TODAY? _____

....

....

....

....

fuel

❑ PROTEIN WITH EACH MEAL
❑ COLOR WITH EACH MEAL
WHAT COLORS DID I EAT TODAY? ....
WATER INTAKE.. HOW MANY OUNCES DID I DRINK TODAY? ....
❑ GAVE MY BODY A FOOD REST BEFORE BED SO IT IS ABLE TO FOCUS
ON RESTORING AND REPAIRING WHILE I SLEEP

reflection

    WAS THIS A REALLY GOOD DAY? WHAT DID I LOVE ABOUT
TODAY? WHAT DO I WANT TO BE BETTER WITH TOMORROW?

....

....

....

....

date ————————————————————————

FIND YOUR FIRE

- UNKNOWN

HOW MUCH SLEEP DID I GET LAST NIGHT? _____

i am so grateful...
3 THINGS I AM GRATEFUL FOR TODAY

1. _____
2. _____
3. _____

what fires you up...

_____
_____
_____
_____

today's priorities...
3 MOST IMPORTANT THINGS TO DO TODAY:

1. _____
2. _____
3. _____

TODAY I AM THRIVING

evening check in —————————————————

movement

HOW DID I MOVE TODAY? ....

    WEIGHTS❑ HIIT WORKOUT❑ ENJOYED NATURE❑ OTHER❑

HOW WAS MY ENERGY LEVEL TODAY? ....

....

....

....

....

fuel

❑ PROTEIN WITH EACH MEAL
❑ COLOR WITH EACH MEAL
WHAT COLORS DID I EAT TODAY? ....
WATER INTAKE.. HOW MANY OUNCES DID I DRINK TODAY? ....
❑ GAVE MY BODY A FOOD REST BEFORE BED SO IT IS ABLE TO FOCUS
ON RESTORING AND REPAIRING WHILE I SLEEP

reflection

    WAS THIS A REALLY GOOD DAY? WHAT DID I LOVE ABOUT
    TODAY? WHAT DO I WANT TO BE BETTER WITH TOMORROW?

....

....

....

....

TODAY I AM THRIVING

date _____

DARE TO LIVE THE LIFE YOU
HAVE ALWAYS WANTED
- RALPH WALDO EMERSON

HOW MUCH SLEEP DID I GET LAST NIGHT?_____

i am so grateful...
3 THINGS I AM GRATEFUL FOR TODAY

1. _____
2. _____
3. _____

what is something you want to add into your life...

_____
_____
_____
_____

today's priorities...
3 MOST IMPORTANT THINGS TO DO TODAY:

1. _____
2. _____
3. _____

evening check in

movement

HOW DID I MOVE TODAY? _____

    WEIGHTS❑ HIIT WORKOUT❑ ENJOYED NATURE❑ OTHER❑

HOW WAS MY ENERGY LEVEL TODAY? _____

_____
_____
_____
_____

fuel

    ❑ PROTEIN WITH EACH MEAL
    ❑ COLOR WITH EACH MEAL
WHAT COLORS DID I EAT TODAY? _____
WATER INTAKE.. HOW MANY OUNCES DID I DRINK TODAY? _____
❑ GAVE MY BODY A FOOD REST BEFORE BED SO IT IS ABLE TO FOCUS
ON RESTORING AND REPAIRING WHILE I SLEEP

reflection

    WAS THIS A REALLY GOOD DAY? WHAT DID I LOVE ABOUT
    TODAY? WHAT DO I WANT TO BE BETTER WITH TOMORROW?

_____
_____
_____
_____

TODAY I AM THRIVING

date _____

ALWAYS TAKE THE SCENIC ROUTE

- UNKNOWN

HOW MUCH SLEEP DID I GET LAST NIGHT? _____

i am so grateful...

3 THINGS I AM GRATEFUL FOR TODAY

1. _____
2. _____
3. _____

what is something new i can do today...

_____

_____

_____

_____

today's priorities...

3 MOST IMPORTANT THINGS TO DO TODAY:

1. _____
2. _____
3. _____

evening check in

movement

HOW DID I MOVE TODAY? _____

WEIGHTS❑ HIIT WORKOUT❑ ENJOYED NATURE❑ OTHER❑

HOW WAS MY ENERGY LEVEL TODAY? _____

_____

_____

_____

_____

fuel

❑ PROTEIN WITH EACH MEAL
❑ COLOR WITH EACH MEAL
WHAT COLORS DID I EAT TODAY? _____
WATER INTAKE.. HOW MANY OUNCES DID I DRINK TODAY? _____
❑ GAVE MY BODY A FOOD REST BEFORE BED SO IT IS ABLE TO FOCUS
ON RESTORING AND REPAIRING WHILE I SLEEP

reflection

WAS THIS A REALLY GOOD DAY? WHAT DID I LOVE ABOUT
TODAY? WHAT DO I WANT TO BE BETTER WITH TOMORROW?

_____

_____

_____

_____

date _____

YOU DON'T HAVE TO CONTROL YOUR THOUGHTS; YOU JUST HAVE TO STOP LETTING THEM CONTROL YOU

- DAN MILLMAN

HOW MUCH SLEEP DID I GET LAST NIGHT? _____

i am so grateful...

3 THINGS I AM GRATEFUL FOR TODAY

1. _____
2. _____
3. _____

what are you most proud of right now...

_____
_____
_____
_____

today's priorities...

3 MOST IMPORTANT THINGS TO DO TODAY:

1. _____
2. _____
3. _____

evening check in ————————————

movement

HOW DID I MOVE TODAY? ....

WEIGHTS❑ HIIT WORKOUT❑ ENJOYED NATURE❑ OTHER❑

HOW WAS MY ENERGY LEVEL TODAY? ....

....

....

....

....

fuel

❑ PROTEIN WITH EACH MEAL
❑ COLOR WITH EACH MEAL
WHAT COLORS DID I EAT TODAY? ....
WATER INTAKE.. HOW MANY OUNCES DID I DRINK TODAY? ....
❑ GAVE MY BODY A FOOD REST BEFORE BED SO IT IS ABLE TO FOCUS
ON RESTORING AND REPAIRING WHILE I SLEEP

reflection

WAS THIS A REALLY GOOD DAY? WHAT DID I LOVE ABOUT
TODAY? WHAT DO I WANT TO BE BETTER WITH TOMORROW?

....

....

....

....

date _____

YESTERDAY IS HISTORY. TOMORROW IS MYSTERY. TODAY IS A GIFT. THAT'S WHY WE CALL IT "THE PRESENT'

– ELEANOR ROOSEVELT

HOW MUCH SLEEP DID I GET LAST NIGHT? _____

i am so grateful...

3 THINGS I AM GRATEFUL FOR TODAY

1. _____
2. _____
3. _____

how can i be more present today...

_____
_____
_____
_____

today's priorities...

3 MOST IMPORTANT THINGS TO DO TODAY:

1. _____
2. _____
3. _____

evening check in

movement

HOW DID I MOVE TODAY? ....

    WEIGHTS❑ HIIT WORKOUT❑ ENJOYED NATURE❑ OTHER❑

HOW WAS MY ENERGY LEVEL TODAY? ....

....

....

....

....

fuel

❑ PROTEIN WITH EACH MEAL
❑ COLOR WITH EACH MEAL
WHAT COLORS DID I EAT TODAY? ....
WATER INTAKE.. HOW MANY OUNCES DID I DRINK TODAY? ....
❑ GAVE MY BODY A FOOD REST BEFORE BED SO IT IS ABLE TO FOCUS
ON RESTORING AND REPAIRING WHILE I SLEEP

reflection

    WAS THIS A REALLY GOOD DAY? WHAT DID I LOVE ABOUT
TODAY? WHAT DO I WANT TO BE BETTER WITH TOMORROW?

....

....

....

....

TODAY I AM THRIVING

date _____

WHEN THINGS CHANGE INSIDE YOU,
THINGS CHANGE AROUND YOU

- UNKNOWN

HOW MUCH SLEEP DID I GET LAST NIGHT? _____

i am so grateful...

3 THINGS I AM GRATEFUL FOR TODAY

1. _____
2. _____
3. _____

what changes have i noticed since starting this journal...

_____
_____
_____
_____

today's priorities...

3 MOST IMPORTANT THINGS TO DO TODAY:

1. _____
2. _____
3. _____

TODAY I AM THRIVING

evening check in

movement

HOW DID I MOVE TODAY? ....

    WEIGHTS❑ HIIT WORKOUT❑ ENJOYED NATURE❑ OTHER❑

HOW WAS MY ENERGY LEVEL TODAY? ....

....
....
....
....

fuel

❑ PROTEIN WITH EACH MEAL
❑ COLOR WITH EACH MEAL
WHAT COLORS DID I EAT TODAY? ....
WATER INTAKE.. HOW MANY OUNCES DID I DRINK TODAY? ....
❑ GAVE MY BODY A FOOD REST BEFORE BED SO IT IS ABLE TO FOCUS
ON RESTORING AND REPAIRING WHILE I SLEEP

reflection

    WAS THIS A REALLY GOOD DAY? WHAT DID I LOVE ABOUT
    TODAY? WHAT DO I WANT TO BE BETTER WITH TOMORROW?

....
....
....
....

TODAY I AM THRIVING

weekly reflection

HOW MANY REALLY GOOD DAYS DID I HAVE THIS WEEK? WHAT DO I WANT TO WORK ON NEXT WEEK?

_____

_____

_____

_____

_____

_____

_____

_____

_____

_____

_____

_____

_____

_____

_____

TODAY I AM THRIVING

date _____

A MONTH FROM NOW YOU CAN
EITHER HAVE A MONTH OF PROGRESS
OR A MONTH OF EXCUSES

- UNKNOWN

HOW MUCH SLEEP DID I GET LAST NIGHT? ....

i am so grateful...

3 THINGS I AM GRATEFUL FOR TODAY

1. ....
2. ....
3. ....

what do i want to start today...

....
....
....
....

today's priorities...

3 MOST IMPORTANT THINGS TO DO TODAY:

1. ....
2. ....
3. ....

TODAY I AM THRIVING

evening check in

movement

HOW DID I MOVE TODAY? ....

WEIGHTS❑ HIIT WORKOUT❑ ENJOYED NATURE❑ OTHER❑

HOW WAS MY ENERGY LEVEL TODAY? ....

....

....

....

....

fuel

❑ PROTEIN WITH EACH MEAL
❑ COLOR WITH EACH MEAL
WHAT COLORS DID I EAT TODAY? _____
WATER INTAKE.. HOW MANY OUNCES DID I DRINK TODAY? ....
❑ GAVE MY BODY A FOOD REST BEFORE BED SO IT IS ABLE TO FOCUS
ON RESTORING AND REPAIRING WHILE I SLEEP

reflection

WAS THIS A REALLY GOOD DAY? WHAT DID I LOVE ABOUT
TODAY? WHAT DO I WANT TO BE BETTER WITH TOMORROW?

....

....

....

....

TODAY I AM THRIVING

date _____

IN TWO WEEKS YOU WILL FEEL IT.
IN FOUR WEEKS YOU WILL SEE IT.
IN SIX WEEKS YOU WILL HEAR IT

-- UNKNOWN

HOW MUCH SLEEP DID I GET LAST NIGHT? ....

i am so grateful...
3 THINGS I AM GRATEFUL FOR TODAY

1. ....
2. ....
3. ....

what changes am i noticing since adding in a few new habits...

....
....
....
....

today's priorities...
3 MOST IMPORTANT THINGS TO DO TODAY:

1. ....
2. ....
3. ....

TODAY I AM THRIVING

evening check in

movement

HOW DID I MOVE TODAY? ....

WEIGHTS❏ HIIT WORKOUT❏ ENJOYED NATURE❏ OTHER❏

HOW WAS MY ENERGY LEVEL TODAY? ....

....
....
....
....

fuel

❏ PROTEIN WITH EACH MEAL
❏ COLOR WITH EACH MEAL
WHAT COLORS DID I EAT TODAY? ....
WATER INTAKE.. HOW MANY OUNCES DID I DRINK TODAY? ....
❏ GAVE MY BODY A FOOD REST BEFORE BED SO IT IS ABLE TO FOCUS
ON RESTORING AND REPAIRING WHILE I SLEEP

reflection

WAS THIS A REALLY GOOD DAY? WHAT DID I LOVE ABOUT
TODAY? WHAT DO I WANT TO BE BETTER WITH TOMORROW?

....
....
....
....

TODAY I AM THRIVING

date —————————————————————————

THE LIFE IN FRONT OF YOU IS FAR MORE IMPORTANT THAN THE LIFE BEHIND YOU
- JOEL OSTEEN

HOW MUCH SLEEP DID I GET LAST NIGHT?_____

i am so grateful...
3 THINGS I AM GRATEFUL FOR TODAY

1. ....
2. ....
3. ....

what are you most excited about right now...

....

....

....

....

TODAY'S PRIORITIES... 3 MOST IMPORTANT THINGS TO DO TODAY:

1. ....
2. ....
3. ....

evening check in ——————————————————————

movement

HOW DID I MOVE TODAY? _____

WEIGHTS❑ HIIT WORKOUT❑ ENJOYED NATURE❑ OTHER❑

HOW WAS MY ENERGY LEVEL TODAY? _____

_____
_____
_____
_____

fuel

❑ PROTEIN WITH EACH MEAL
❑ COLOR WITH EACH MEAL
WHAT COLORS DID I EAT TODAY? _____
WATER INTAKE.. HOW MANY OUNCES DID I DRINK TODAY? _____
❑ GAVE MY BODY A FOOD REST BEFORE BED SO IT IS ABLE TO FOCUS
ON RESTORING AND REPAIRING WHILE I SLEEP

reflection

WAS THIS A REALLY GOOD DAY? WHAT DID I LOVE ABOUT
TODAY? WHAT DO I WANT TO BE BETTER WITH TOMORROW?

_____
_____
_____
_____

TODAY I AM THRIVING

date ————————————————————

YOUR POTENTIAL IS ENDLESS
— MARIA FORLEO

HOW MUCH SLEEP DID I GET LAST NIGHT?...

i am so grateful...
3 THINGS I AM GRATEFUL FOR TODAY

1. ....
2. ....
3. ....

what am i most passionate about right now...

....

....

....

today's priorities...
3 MOST IMPORTANT THINGS TO DO TODAY:

1. ....
2. ....
3. ....

evening check in

movement

HOW DID I MOVE TODAY? _____

WEIGHTS❑ HIIT WORKOUT❑ ENJOYED NATURE❑ OTHER❑

HOW WAS MY ENERGY LEVEL TODAY? _____

_____
_____
_____
_____

fuel

❑ PROTEIN WITH EACH MEAL
❑ COLOR WITH EACH MEAL
WHAT COLORS DID I EAT TODAY? _____
WATER INTAKE.. HOW MANY OUNCES DID I DRINK TODAY? _____
❑ GAVE MY BODY A FOOD REST BEFORE BED SO IT IS ABLE TO FOCUS
ON RESTORING AND REPAIRING WHILE I SLEEP

reflection

WAS THIS A REALLY GOOD DAY? WHAT DID I LOVE ABOUT
TODAY? WHAT DO I WANT TO BE BETTER WITH TOMORROW?

_____
_____
_____
_____

TODAY I AM THRIVING

date _____

FILL YOU LIFE WITH
ADVENTURES NOT THINGS

- TINY BUDDHA

HOW MUCH SLEEP DID I GET LAST NIGHT? _____

i am so grateful...
3 THINGS I AM GRATEFUL FOR TODAY

1. _____
2. _____
3. _____

what are some new adventures i want to focus on doing...

_____

_____

_____

_____

today's priorities...
3 MOST IMPORTANT THINGS TO DO TODAY:

1. _____
2. _____
3. _____

evening check in

movement

HOW DID I MOVE TODAY? ....

WEIGHTS❑ HIIT WORKOUT❑ ENJOYED NATURE❑ OTHER❑

HOW WAS MY ENERGY LEVEL TODAY? ....

....

....

....

....

fuel

❑ PROTEIN WITH EACH MEAL
❑ COLOR WITH EACH MEAL
WHAT COLORS DID I EAT TODAY? ....
WATER INTAKE.. HOW MANY OUNCES DID I DRINK TODAY? ....
❑ GAVE MY BODY A FOOD REST BEFORE BED SO IT IS ABLE TO FOCUS
ON RESTORING AND REPAIRING WHILE I SLEEP

reflection

WAS THIS A REALLY GOOD DAY? WHAT DID I LOVE ABOUT
TODAY? WHAT DO I WANT TO BE BETTER WITH TOMORROW?

....

....

....

....

TODAY I AM THRIVING

date _____

YOU ARE WHAT YOU EAT SO DON'T BE FAST, CHEAP, EASY OR FAKE

- UNKNOWN

HOW MUCH SLEEP DID I GET LAST NIGHT? _____

i am so grateful...

3 THINGS I AM GRATEFUL FOR TODAY

1. _____
2. _____
3. _____

what do you like most about the perspective that food is medicine...

_____

_____

_____

_____

today's priorities...

3 MOST IMPORTANT THINGS TO DO TODAY:

1. _____
2. _____
3. _____

evening check in

movement

HOW DID I MOVE TODAY? _____

WEIGHTS❑ HIIT WORKOUT❑ ENJOYED NATURE❑ OTHER❑

HOW WAS MY ENERGY LEVEL TODAY? _____

_____
_____
_____
_____

fuel

❑ PROTEIN WITH EACH MEAL
❑ COLOR WITH EACH MEAL
WHAT COLORS DID I EAT TODAY? _____
WATER INTAKE.. HOW MANY OUNCES DID I DRINK TODAY? _____
❑ GAVE MY BODY A FOOD REST BEFORE BED SO IT IS ABLE TO FOCUS
ON RESTORING AND REPAIRING WHILE I SLEEP

reflection

WAS THIS A REALLY GOOD DAY? WHAT DID I LOVE ABOUT
TODAY? WHAT DO I WANT TO BE BETTER WITH TOMORROW?

_____
_____
_____
_____

TODAY I AM THRIVING

date ————————————————————————

DO WHAT MAKES YOUR SOUL SHINE
- UNKNOWN

HOW MUCH SLEEP DID I GET LAST NIGHT? _____

i am so grateful...
3 THINGS I AM GRATEFUL FOR TODAY

1. _____
2. _____
3. _____

what are your favorite things to do and are you doing them...

_____

_____

_____

_____

today's priorities...
3 MOST IMPORTANT THINGS TO DO TODAY:

1. _____
2. _____
3. _____

—— *evening check in* ——————————————————

movement

HOW DID I MOVE TODAY? ....

WEIGHTS❑ HIIT WORKOUT❑ ENJOYED NATURE❑ OTHER❑

HOW WAS MY ENERGY LEVEL TODAY? ....

....
....
....
....

fuel

❑ PROTEIN WITH EACH MEAL
❑ COLOR WITH EACH MEAL
WHAT COLORS DID I EAT TODAY? _____
WATER INTAKE.. HOW MANY OUNCES DID I DRINK TODAY? _____
❑ GAVE MY BODY A FOOD REST BEFORE BED SO IT IS ABLE TO FOCUS
ON RESTORING AND REPAIRING WHILE I SLEEP

reflection

WAS THIS A REALLY GOOD DAY? WHAT DID I LOVE ABOUT
TODAY? WHAT DO I WANT TO BE BETTER WITH TOMORROW?

....
....
....
....

weekly reflection

HOW MANY REALLY GOOD DAYS DID I HAVE THIS WEEK? WHAT DO I WANT TO WORK ON NEXT WEEK?

date _____

ENJOY THE LITTLE THINGS IN LIFE. FOR ONE DAY YOU WILL LOOK BACK AND REALIZE THEY WERE THE BIG THINGS

- KURT VONNEGUT JR

HOW MUCH SLEEP DID I GET LAST NIGHT? _____

i am so grateful...

3 THINGS I AM GRATEFUL FOR TODAY

1. _____
2. _____
3. _____

the best version of me is...

_____
_____
_____
_____

today's priorities...

3 MOST IMPORTANT THINGS TO DO TODAY:

1. _____
2. _____
3. _____

evening check in

movement

HOW DID I MOVE TODAY? ....

WEIGHTS❑ HIIT WORKOUT❑ ENJOYED NATURE❑ OTHER❑

HOW WAS MY ENERGY LEVEL TODAY? ....

....
....
....
....

fuel

❑ PROTEIN WITH EACH MEAL
❑ COLOR WITH EACH MEAL
WHAT COLORS DID I EAT TODAY? ....
WATER INTAKE.. HOW MANY OUNCES DID I DRINK TODAY? ....
❑ GAVE MY BODY A FOOD REST BEFORE BED SO IT IS ABLE TO FOCUS
ON RESTORING AND REPAIRING WHILE I SLEEP

reflection

WAS THIS A REALLY GOOD DAY? WHAT DID I LOVE ABOUT
TODAY? WHAT DO I WANT TO BE BETTER WITH TOMORROW?

....
....
....
....

date _____

BETTER AN "OOPS' THAN A "WHAT IF"

-- UNKNOWN

HOW MUCH SLEEP DID I GET LAST NIGHT? _____

i am so grateful...

3 THINGS I AM GRATEFUL FOR TODAY

1. _____
2. _____
3. _____

what have i been putting off...

_____
_____
_____

today's priorities...

3 MOST IMPORTANT THINGS TO DO TODAY:

1. _____
2. _____
3. _____

evening check in

movement

HOW DID I MOVE TODAY? ....

WEIGHTS☐ HIIT WORKOUT☐ ENJOYED NATURE☐ OTHER☐

HOW WAS MY ENERGY LEVEL TODAY? ....

....
....
....
....

fuel

☐ PROTEIN WITH EACH MEAL
☐ COLOR WITH EACH MEAL
WHAT COLORS DID I EAT TODAY? ....
WATER INTAKE.. HOW MANY OUNCES DID I DRINK TODAY? ....
☐ GAVE MY BODY A FOOD REST BEFORE BED SO IT IS ABLE TO FOCUS
ON RESTORING AND REPAIRING WHILE I SLEEP

reflection

WAS THIS A REALLY GOOD DAY? WHAT DID I LOVE ABOUT
TODAY? WHAT DO I WANT TO BE BETTER WITH TOMORROW?

....
....
....
....

TODAY I AM THRIVING

date _____

DO SOMETHING TODAY YOUR FUTURE
SELF WILL THANK YOU FOR

- SEAN PATRICK FLANERY

HOW MUCH SLEEP DID I GET LAST NIGHT?_____

i am so grateful...
3 THINGS I AM GRATEFUL FOR TODAY

1. _____
2. _____
3. _____

what is something you want to accomplish this month...

_____
_____
_____
_____

today's priorities...
3 MOST IMPORTANT THINGS TO DO TODAY:

1. _____
2. _____
3. _____

evening check in

movement

HOW DID I MOVE TODAY? ....

    WEIGHTS❑ HIIT WORKOUT❑ ENJOYED NATURE❑ OTHER❑

HOW WAS MY ENERGY LEVEL TODAY? ....

....

....

....

....

fuel

❑ PROTEIN WITH EACH MEAL
❑ COLOR WITH EACH MEAL
WHAT COLORS DID I EAT TODAY? ....
WATER INTAKE.. HOW MANY OUNCES DID I DRINK TODAY? ....
❑ GAVE MY BODY A FOOD REST BEFORE BED SO IT IS ABLE TO FOCUS
ON RESTORING AND REPAIRING WHILE I SLEEP

reflection

    WAS THIS A REALLY GOOD DAY? WHAT DID I LOVE ABOUT
    TODAY? WHAT DO I WANT TO BE BETTER WITH TOMORROW?

....

....

....

....

date _____

THE PAST IS OUR LESSON. THE PRESENT IS YOUR GIFT. THE FUTURE IS YOUR MOTIVATION

- MALENE DEGN

HOW MUCH SLEEP DID I GET LAST NIGHT? _____

i am so grateful...

3 THINGS I AM GRATEFUL FOR TODAY

1. _____
2. _____
3. _____

what are some of my biggest life lessons...

_____

_____

_____

_____

today's priorities...

3 MOST IMPORTANT THINGS TO DO TODAY:

1. _____
2. _____
3. _____

evening check in

movement

HOW DID I MOVE TODAY? ....

WEIGHTS❑ HIIT WORKOUT❑ ENJOYED NATURE❑ OTHER❑

HOW WAS MY ENERGY LEVEL TODAY? ....

....
....
....
....

fuel

❑ PROTEIN WITH EACH MEAL
❑ COLOR WITH EACH MEAL
WHAT COLORS DID I EAT TODAY? ....
WATER INTAKE.. HOW MANY OUNCES DID I DRINK TODAY? ....
❑ GAVE MY BODY A FOOD REST BEFORE BED SO IT IS ABLE TO FOCUS
ON RESTORING AND REPAIRING WHILE I SLEEP

reflection

WAS THIS A REALLY GOOD DAY? WHAT DID I LOVE ABOUT
TODAY? WHAT DO I WANT TO BE BETTER WITH TOMORROW?

....
....
....
....

TODAY I AM THRIVING

date _____

WHATEVER YOU DECIDE TO DO,
MAKE SURE IT MAKES YOU HAPPY

- PAULO COELHO

HOW MUCH SLEEP DID I GET LAST NIGHT? _____

i am so grateful...
3 THINGS I AM GRATEFUL FOR TODAY

1. _____
2. _____
3. _____

what makes me happy...

_____
_____
_____
_____

today's priorities...
3 MOST IMPORTANT THINGS TO DO TODAY:

1. _____
2. _____
3. _____

evening check in

movement

HOW DID I MOVE TODAY? ....

     WEIGHTS❏ HIIT WORKOUT❏ ENJOYED NATURE❏ OTHER❏

HOW WAS MY ENERGY LEVEL TODAY? _____

_____

_____

_____

_____

fuel

❏ PROTEIN WITH EACH MEAL
❏ COLOR WITH EACH MEAL
WHAT COLORS DID I EAT TODAY? _____
WATER INTAKE.. HOW MANY OUNCES DID I DRINK TODAY? _____
❏ GAVE MY BODY A FOOD REST BEFORE BED SO IT IS ABLE TO FOCUS
ON RESTORING AND REPAIRING WHILE I SLEEP

reflection

    WAS THIS A REALLY GOOD DAY? WHAT DID I LOVE ABOUT
    TODAY? WHAT DO I WANT TO BE BETTER WITH TOMORROW?

_____

_____

_____

_____

TODAY I AM THRIVING

date _____

YOUR HEALTH IS YOUR GREATEST WEALTH

- UNKNOWN

HOW MUCH SLEEP DID I GET LAST NIGHT? _____

i am so grateful...

3 THINGS I AM GRATEFUL FOR TODAY

1. _____
2. _____
3. _____

i feel my best when....

_____
_____
_____
_____

today's priorities...

3 MOST IMPORTANT THINGS TO DO TODAY:

1. _____
2. _____
3. _____

evening check in

movement

HOW DID I MOVE TODAY? ....

WEIGHTS❑ HIIT WORKOUT❑ ENJOYED NATURE❑ OTHER❑

HOW WAS MY ENERGY LEVEL TODAY? _____

....

....

....

....

fuel

❑ PROTEIN WITH EACH MEAL
❑ COLOR WITH EACH MEAL
WHAT COLORS DID I EAT TODAY? ....
WATER INTAKE.. HOW MANY OUNCES DID I DRINK TODAY? ....
❑ GAVE MY BODY A FOOD REST BEFORE BED SO IT IS ABLE TO FOCUS
ON RESTORING AND REPAIRING WHILE I SLEEP

reflection

WAS THIS A REALLY GOOD DAY? WHAT DID I LOVE ABOUT
TODAY? WHAT DO I WANT TO BE BETTER WITH TOMORROW?

....

....

....

....

TODAY I AM THRIVING

CONGRATULATIONS! YOU DID IT! You finished your 90 day journey. I am so proud of you. Take some time to reflect. How are you feeling? How many good days and weeks have you had? What new habits have you incorporated that you plan to continue? Spend some time thinking about this next chapter that you will create if you continue focusing on the things you have learned in this journal. Cheers to you and to making the rest of your life the best part of your life.

Would love to stay in touch with you.
IG @shannonblas
www.thrivingto50andbeyond.com

Printed in the United States
by Baker & Taylor Publisher Services